Undocumented Immigration to California: 1980–1993

. . .

Hans P. Johnson

SEPTEMBER 1996

PUBLIC POLICY INSTITUTE OF CALIFORNIA

Library of Congress Cataloging-in-Publication Data
Johnson, Hans P.
    Undocumented immigration to California. 1980—1993 / Hans P.
Johnson.
            p.   cm.
    Originally published: San Francisco, CA: Public Policy Institute
of California, 1996.
    Includes bibliographical references (p.   ).
    ISBN: 0-9653184-1-9 (pbk.)
    1. Illegal aliens California Statistics. 2. Illegal aliens
California History 20th century. 3. California Emigration and
immigration Statistics. 4. California Emigration and
immigration History 20th century. 5. California Economic
conditions. I. Title.
JV6920.J64   1997   97-29763
304.8794 009 048 dc21   CIP

Research publications reflect the views of the authors and do not
necessarily reflect the views of the staff, officers, or Board of
Directors of the Public Policy Institute of California.

Foreword

As so often in California's past, immigration is currently the focus of intense public debate. Whether the issue is labor force substitution, assimilation, bilingual education, social services, multiculturalism, or undocumented workers, opinions are plentiful but facts are not. In the central policy debate over the costs and benefits of immigration, there is a need for reliable estimates of the annual flow of undocumented immigrants into and out of the state—especially given the unprecedented increase in California's population in the 1980s.

This report, by research fellow Hans Johnson, provides the first systematic estimates of net annual undocumented immigration to California. Estimating undocumented immigration flows is fraught with uncertainty—about the level of total population due to census undercount, about domestic migration, and about the flow of legal immigration. The author makes explicit a set of assumptions about these and other components of population change, and then shows that, for a thirteen-year period, net annual undocumented immigration follows a pattern different from that previously assumed and that the flow changed dramatically between the early 1980s and the early 1990s.

These findings provide a new perspective on undocumented immigration to California. The fluctuation of immigration over time suggests a connection to the state's economy and to policy interventions such as the Immigration Reform and Control Act of 1986. The findings also suggest that the consequences of policy intervention are not easy to predict. But we now have a systematic methodology for monitoring this very important component of population change, and the first estimates necessary to evaluate the consequences of policy intervention in future years.

The author expresses his gratitude to Mary Heim, Greg Robinson, and Karen Woodrow-Lafield for their extensive and helpful comments on an earlier version of the study. The Demographic Research Unit of the California Department of Finance has generously provided data and expertise. Gary Bjork and John Ellwood provided considerable editorial and production assistance. The study has benefited from the comments and contributions of numerous colleagues, particularly Belinda Reyes, Sonya Tafoya, and Paul Lewis. While this report reflects the contributions of many people, the author is solely responsible for its content.

David W. Lyon
President and CEO
Public Policy Institute of California

Summary

Over the past several decades, California's population has experienced extraordinary growth and diversification. In the 1980s alone, the state gained over six million new residents; according to the findings of this study, between 22 percent and 31 percent of these newcomers were undocumented immigrants. California leads every state in the nation as a destination for undocumented immigrants. The Immigration and Naturalization Service (INS) estimates that almost half of the undocumented immigrant population in the United States resides in California.

While undocumented immigration is a central focus of many of California's public policy debates, demographers have found it difficult to develop precise population estimates of undocumented immigrants. Estimation of annual changes in the population of undocumented immigrants is even more difficult, with current estimates of change providing little state-level information, if any. This study represents the first systematic effort to develop annual estimates of the net migration of undocumented immigrants to California. The study develops estimates from 1980 through 1993.

Traditional Estimating Procedures

Various methods have been used to indirectly estimate the number of undocumented immigrants in the United States. Most of the current estimates are based on a residual method. Such estimates are generally derived by subtracting the number of legal immigrants residing in the country from the number of foreign-born persons counted in a census or survey. The difference, or residual, is attributed to undocumented immigration. Adjustments are made to account for misreporting of place of birth, emigration, and mortality.

State estimates are often derived from national estimates using various measures of distribution of foreign-born persons across states. Average annual changes in the undocumented immigrant population within the state are then obtained by calculating the difference between stock estimates from two points in time. Some researchers derive state estimates for multiyear periods directly from census and INS data. For California, the traditional estimating procedure suggests that annual changes in the state's population due to undocumented immigration averaged 100,000 in the 1980s and 125,000 in the 1990s.

Revised Methodology

The study reported here for California also uses a residual method, but in this case the estimation procedure is based on an analysis of the annual components of population change—births, deaths, and net migration. Net migration comprises net legal immigration, net domestic migration (i.e., migration to and from other states), and net undocumented immigration.

A two-step process is used to create annual net estimates of undocumented immigration (i.e., the difference between those who immigrate into the state and those who emigrate out of the state).

In the first step, the total change in the number of people living in California between 1980 and 1993 is calculated: Total population change in California is estimated for the decade of the 1980s based on 1980 and 1990 censuses; then annual estimates of population change between 1980 and 1993 are developed using various indicators of population size (e.g., occupied housing units, driver licenses, school enrollment, births, deaths, and Medicare enrollment).

In the second step, estimates of the components of population change are developed, with net undocumented immigration serving as the residual after all other components are taken into account.

Because the estimates of population change and the estimates of the components of population change are subject to uncertainty, precise point estimates of annual net undocumented immigration are not possible. In order to evaluate the sensitivity of the undocumented immigration estimates to this uncertainty, over thirty series of annual net undocumented immigration estimates are developed. Each of the series incorporates various assumptions about annual population change and the components of population change. While differences between the estimates for any one year are large, each of the series suggests the same general pattern over time. Thus, while any point estimate of net undocumented immigration for a particular year is not reliable, the range of estimates for most years is reliable and the pattern over time is robust.

Patterns of Undocumented Immigration

The estimates of net undocumented immigration between 1980 and 1993 suggest low levels of undocumented immigration during the early 1980s, high levels during the late 1980s, and a dramatic downturn in the early 1990s. Each of the series of estimates of net undocumented immigration developed in this report shows the same general pattern. Figure S.1 shows six estimates for each year based on alternative assumptions about annual population change. Specifically, the following patterns emerge:

- 1980 to 1985. Net undocumented immigration to California was at a relatively low level during the early 1980s. Between 1980 and 1985, net undocumented immigration averaged less than 100,000 persons per year.

- 1986 to 1989. Net undocumented immigration rose throughout the middle of the 1980s, reaching a peak of well over 200,000 persons between April 1989 and April 1990. Because these are net estimates, this increase could result from fewer undocumented immigrants leaving the state, from an increase in the number of undocumented immigrants entering the state, or from a combination of both.

- 1990 to 1993. A sharp decline in net undocumented immigration to California has occurred since 1990, so that by 1992–1993, the net flow of undocumented immigrants to the state may have declined to less than 100,000 per year.

These patterns indicate that net undocumented immigration fluctuates widely over time. In particular, this study finds that between 1980 and 1993 changes in the net flow of undocumented immigrants coincide with and contribute to periods of both rapid and slow population growth in the state.

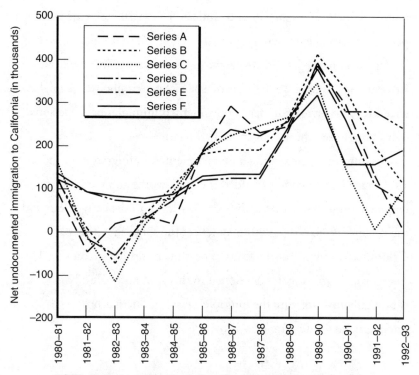

NOTE: Estimates derived from alternative scenarios of population change. Series A population change based primarily on licensed drivers; Series B based primarily on occupied households; Series C based primarily on persons per household; Series D is an average of Series A, B, and C; Series E and Series F are based on California Department of Finance and U.S. Bureau of the Census estimates of population change. See Appendix A for a discussion of the development of the population change estimates.

Figure S.1—Estimates of Net Undocumented Immigration to California

Possible Explanations

California's economic conditions may have contributed to the migration patterns. Low levels of net undocumented immigration do coincide with slow employment growth in California in the early 1980s, and the decline in estimated net undocumented immigration in the early 1990s coincides with the state's most recent recession. High levels of net undocumented immigration in the mid to late 1980s coincide with periods of strong employment growth. The peak in undocumented immigration in the late 1980s might be related to the Immigration Reform and Control Act (IRCA) of 1986. Specifically, IRCA might have led to an increase in net undocumented immigration as persons living abroad sought to join amnestied relatives.

In sum, the increase in net undocumented immigration in the late 1980s may be related to expanded social networks and plentiful employment opportunities, while the low levels in the early 1980s and the decline in the early 1990s may reflect the sluggish nature of California's economy at the time. These relationships are only suggestive. The estimates developed in this study provide a base for thoroughly investigating the multiple causes of fluctuating undocumented immigrant flows over time.

Contents

Figures

Tables

1. Introduction

California has one of the most diverse and rapidly growing populations in the developed world. The state's population growth and its composition have led to numerous public policy debates across a wide range of issues, including education, housing, political representation, and growth management. Most recently, although with substantial precedence at various times in California's history, much of the debate has centered on immigration. In particular, *undocumented* immigration has come to dominate the political discussion about population in California.[1] While much of this debate has centered on fiscal issues (whether undocumented immigrants pay less in taxes than they receive in

---

[1]The terms undocumented immigration, illegal immigration, and unauthorized immigration have been used interchangeably to describe the phenomenon of international migration to the United States in violation of federal immigration law. We use the terms undocumented immigration and undocumented immigrants following the terminology used by the U.S. Bureau of the Census in its recent population estimates (see, for example, *Current Population Reports*, P25-1127; and Fernandez and Robinson, 1994).

services),[2] other areas of concern include effects on wages and employment, contribution to the state's work force in terms of skills and education, and links between international migration and domestic migration.

Debates about the effects of undocumented immigration continue, but a fundamental measure of any population—annual changes in the size of that population—remains elusive in the case of undocumented immigration. This report represents the first systematic effort to develop estimates of the annual net flow of undocumented immigrants to California.

The primary issue to be addressed in this report is demographic: How many more undocumented immigrants come to California than leave the state each year, and how has that net flow changed over time? The answers to these questions could inform many of the debates on undocumented immigration. If for no other reason, undocumented immigration is an important issue because it is a large and significant component of population growth in California. According to the findings of this report, undocumented immigration accounted for between 22 percent and 31 percent of the state's population growth during the 1980s. California is the leading state of destination for undocumented immigrants, and the Immigration and Naturalization Service (INS) estimates that almost half of the undocumented immigrant population in the United States resides in California (Warren, 1994). Through the use of various data sets and demographic procedures, this

---

[2]See, for example: Clark, Passel, Zimmerman, and Fix (1994); Huddle (1994); Los Angeles County, Internal Services Department, Urban Research Section (1992); Rea and Parker (1992); and Romero and Chang (1994).

report develops estimates of annual net migration of undocumented immigrants to California from 1980 to 1993.

Data and Measurement Issues

The scarcity of credible data on undocumented immigrants has long frustrated researchers attempting to describe and analyze this population. For obvious reasons, undocumented immigrants seek to avoid detection. Undocumented immigrants are not noted as such in administrative data sets. Surveys and censuses do not include questions about the legal status of immigrants. Although the U.S. Census Bureau collects detailed socioeconomic and demographic data in the decennial censuses, the Bureau does not collect information on legal residency status for at least two reasons: (1) a census question on immigration status might discourage undocumented immigrants from participating in the census, and (2) the responses to such a question might not be reliable because some individuals might not know or might misrepresent their own legal status or that of other members of the household.

Demographers, accustomed to working with incomplete data and employing indirect estimation techniques, have been hard-pressed to develop precise population estimates of undocumented immigrants. Definitional issues compound the problems created by the lack of data. Should persons who overstay their visas for a few weeks be included in estimates of undocumented immigrants? What about unauthorized border crossers who use false documents to travel to the United States for a few days?

In this study, we sought to count undocumented immigrant *residents* of the United States. Semi-permanent and permanent undocumented

3

immigrant residents are likely to have the greatest impact in those areas of most concern to policymakers.

Various methodologies have been used to indirectly estimate the number of undocumented immigrants in the United States. Most of the current estimates are based on a residual method (see, for example, Passel and Woodrow, 1984; Passel, 1985; Warren and Passel, 1987; Woodrow, 1990; Woodrow and Passel, 1990; and Woodrow, 1992). Generally, such estimates are derived by subtracting the number of legal immigrants residing in the country (based on INS data) from the number of foreign-born persons counted in a census or survey. The difference, or residual, is attributed to undocumented immigration. Adjustments are made to account for misreporting of place of birth, emigration, and mortality. State estimates, when developed, are generally based on national estimates and are determined by using various measures of the distribution of foreign-born persons across states.[3] Estimates of multiyear average annual change in the undocumented immigrant population are determined by examining differences in stock estimates produced from consistent sources and methods at different points in time.

Recent research by the INS, the Census Bureau, and the Urban Institute has produced fairly consistent estimates of the undocumented immigrant population of the United States and California (Warren, 1994; Fernandez and Robinson, 1994; Clark, Passel, Zimmerman, and Fix, 1994).[4] Such estimates, however, have provided little information

---

[3]Exceptions include Clark et al. (1994) and Passel and Woodrow (1984), in which state estimates are determined directly.

[4]Woodrow-Lafield (1995) has developed national estimates that are consistent with the others, but argues for a wider range of plausible estimates.

on annual variations in the net flow of undocumented immigrant residents at the state level.

The approach used in this report, described in the next chapter, also uses a residual approach. In this case, however, the residual is based on an analysis of the annual components of population change (births, deaths, and migration). With the substantial net flows of undocumented immigrants into the state and the availability of unique state-level administrative data to estimate the other components of population change in California, the residual should be of sufficient size to adequately reflect net undocumented immigration to the state.

2. Methodology and Data

This report develops estimates of the annual net migration of undocumented immigrants to California between 1980 and 1993. The estimation procedure is based on an analysis of the components of population change: births, deaths, and net migration. Net migration is composed of net foreign legal immigration, net domestic migration (migration to and from other states), and net undocumented immigration. Administrative records, census data, and Current Population Surveys[1] are used to estimate the various components of California's population change, with a residual category serving as an estimator of undocumented immigration. The study attempts to reconcile differences in estimates produced using the various data sources, and considers the sensitivity of the final results to errors in estimations of any of the components.

---

[1]Conducted monthly by the U.S. Bureau of the Census for the Bureau of Labor Statistics. This report considers the March Current Population Surveys, which include supplemental demographic information.

7

The method used is essentially a two-step process in which total population change is estimated first, and then the components of population change are determined. In the first step, total population change in California is estimated for the decade of the 1980s based on 1980 and 1990 censuses, and annual estimates of total population change between 1980 and 1993 are developed based on various indicators of population size. In the second step, the components of population change are estimated, with net undocumented immigration serving as the residual after all other components of population change are taken into account.

Total population change in California during the 1980s is estimated from census counts of the state's population, with various estimates of the net undercount included in the estimations.[2] Allocation of total population change during the decade to the components of change is uncomplicated in the case of births and deaths, with near universal registration of those vital events. The remainder, after accounting for births and deaths, is net migration. Allocation of net migration to net domestic migration, net foreign legal migration, and net foreign undocumented migration is much more difficult. Coverage and definitional issues complicate the analysis. The estimates of legal foreign in-migration are drawn from tabulations of Immigration and Naturalization Service data. Various estimates of emigration are included in the sensitivity analysis. Other administrative records (driver license address changes from the California Department of Motor Vehicles and tax return migration data from the Internal Revenue Service) provide estimates of domestic migration. Census and Current Population Survey

---

[2]The net undercount is the difference between the total resident population at the time of the census and the census count of the resident population.

data are also used to produce estimates of net domestic migration and gross foreign in-migration. Net undocumented immigration represents the residual component of total net migration, after accounting for net domestic and net legal foreign migration.

This method of estimating net undocumented immigration has several potential advantages over the methods currently used to develop state estimates. The estimate is consistent with estimated population changes at the state level. The method does not rely solely on Current Population Survey data, which have small sample size problems, nor completely on census data, and provides estimates on an annual basis. Numerous data sets are analyzed and evaluated for consistency. The method has disadvantages as well. Because it relies on several estimates of the other components of population change, it is subject to any errors in those estimates. The estimates rely heavily on components for which there is conflicting information. Trends in and broad ranges of net undocumented immigration can be identified, but reliable point estimates are impossible to determine. Also, the residual consists only of estimates of net undocumented immigration, and provides no additional socioeconomic or demographic detail.

The report includes discussions of the annual population estimates and the administrative records used to develop estimates of domestic migration. The plausibility of the point estimates of annual net undocumented immigration is considered, as well as the sensitivity of those estimates to changes in assumptions. A comparison of the estimates produced from the different data sources constitutes a major part of the report. With natural increase and legal immigration relatively well known, the final residual estimates of undocumented immigration depend to a large extent on the estimates of domestic migration and annual population change.

Outline of This Report

Because the estimates of undocumented immigration developed here depend on accurate estimation of population change and the components of population change, the body of this report focuses on the methods and measures used to estimate each of the components of change. Chapter 3 discusses various estimates of total population change both for the decade and for individual years between 1980 and 1993. Total population change from year to year as well as for the decade is one of the most important sources of uncertainty in the final estimates of undocumented immigration. Estimates of natural increase and legal immigration are relatively certain, and are discussed in Chapters 4 and 5. Chapter 5 also considers domestic migration, the other major source of uncertainty in the residual estimates of undocumented immigration. Chapter 6 presents the estimates of undocumented immigration, including tests of the sensitivity of the estimates to changes in assumptions as well as discussions of potential errors. Finally, Chapters 7 and 8 compare the estimates developed here with other estimates and discuss potential explanations for the observed patterns of undocumented immigration.

3. Total Population Change

In order to estimate the components of population change, we must first estimate population change itself, which in turn requires estimates of the total population. After adjusting for undercount, the decennial censuses provide the most accurate count of the state's population. For non-census years we use several estimators of the state's population. Estimates between the years of 1980 and 1990 have the advantage of being bounded by census-based estimates, and are thus more reliable than the post-1990 estimates.

Estimates of Total Population Change for the Decade 1980–1990

Total population change in California between 1980 and 1990 can be estimated using census counts of the population with adjustments made for net undercount.[1] Various assumptions regarding net

---

[1]Because we are attempting to allocate total population change, the undercount is a problem only as it differs in net absolute terms over time.

undercount rates in 1980 and 1990 will produce various estimates of total population change, the extremes of which are implausible (see Table 3.1). For example, it is not reasonable to assume that the 1980 census net undercount was 3.0 percent, whereas the 1990 net undercount was zero; or, more generally, to assume that one census experienced no net undercount whereas the other census experienced a net undercount. On the other hand, the estimates of net undercount in Table 3.1 are not complete—they represent several empirical estimates of the net undercount for California, but do not represent the full range of possible actual net undercount rates.

The magnitude of the impact of net undercount rates on total population change in the decade is a function of both the difference in undercount rates between 1980 and 1990 and the level of the net undercount rate. Table 3.2 provides a matrix of total population change

Table 3.1

California Total Population Change Estimates, 1980–1990

1980 Undercount Adjustment	Census Unadjusted	1990 Undercount Adjustment		
		Census Adjusted per Original PES 3.7%	Census Adjusted per Revised PES 2.7%	Census Adjusted per Synthetic Estimate 2.6%
Census unadjusted	6,092,119	7,220,173	6,926,635	6,886,534
Census adjusted per PEP 3.0%	5,360,122	6,488,176	6,194,638	6,154,537
Census adjusted per synthetic estimate 1.7%	5,682,806	6,810,860	6,517,322	6,477,222

SOURCE: Robinson and Ahmed (1992).

NOTE: PES = Post Enumeration Survey

PEP = Post Enumeration Program

Table 3.2

Alternative Estimates of Total Population Change in California, 1980–1990

(in thousands)

1980 Net Undercount	1990 Net Undercount										
	0.0%	0.5%	1.0%	1.5%	2.0%	2.5%	3.0%	3.5%	4.0%	4.5%	5.0%
0.0%	6,092	6,242	6,393	6,545	6,699	6,855	7,013	7,171	7,332	7,494	7,658
0.5%	5,973	6,123	6,274	6,426	6,581	6,736	6,894	7,053	7,213	7,375	7,540
1.0%	5,853	6,003	6,154	6,306	6,460	6,616	6,773	6,932	7,093	7,255	7,419
1.5%	5,732	5,881	6,032	6,185	6,339	6,495	6,652	6,811	6,972	7,134	7,298
2.0%	5,609	5,759	5,910	6,062	6,216	6,372	6,530	6,688	6,849	7,011	7,175
2.5%	5,485	5,635	5,786	5,938	6,093	6,248	6,406	6,565	6,725	6,888	7,052
3.0%	5,360	5,510	5,661	5,813	5,967	6,123	6,281	6,440	6,600	6,762	6,926
3.5%	5,234	5,383	5,534	5,687	5,841	5,997	6,154	6,313	6,474	6,636	6,800
4.0%	5,106	5,256	5,407	5,559	5,713	5,869	6,026	6,185	6,346	6,508	6,672
4.5%	4,977	5,126	5,277	5,430	5,584	5,740	5,897	6,056	6,217	6,379	6,543
5.0%	4,846	4,996	5,147	5,300	5,454	5,610	5,767	5,926	6,086	6,249	6,413

for California based on various net undercount assumptions. These estimates range from a low of 4.8 million to a high of 7.7 million. This range includes some highly improbable scenarios, and clearly overstates the uncertainty associated with total population change during the decade. Using the empirical estimates of Table 3.1 as a guide, we can place subjective conditions on the scenarios of joint net undercount rates to produce a plausible range of total population change (see Table 3.3).

The first condition places upper and lower bounds on net undercount rates in California. These bounds are between 1.0 percent and 4.0 percent in 1980, and between 1.0 percent and 4.5 percent in 1990, and are based on the empirical estimates shown in Table 3.1, allowing for some error.[2] Table 3.4 provides original and revised 1990 Post Enumeration Survey (PES) estimates, undercount rates, and sampling errors of the undercount rates for California and the United States.

Table 3.3

Estimating Total Population Change in California, 1980–1990

Conditions (Cumulative)	Total Population Change Range
Net undercount rates of between 1.0% and 4.0% in 1980, and between 1.0% and 4.5% in 1990	5.4 million to 7.3 million
Net undercount rates in 1990 at least as high as those of 1980	6.2 million to 7.3 million
Net undercount rates in 1990 no more than twice as high as those of 1980	6.2 million to 6.9 million

[2]For example, as shown in Table 3.4, the original Post Enumeration Survey estimate of the net undercount rate in California in 1990 was 3.65 percent with a standard error of 0.42 percent. The upper bound used in this report for the net undercount in the state's population is 4.5 percent, which is two standard errors above the original PES estimate for the state. The revised PES estimate was substantially lower; thus, the upper bound presented is a generous one.

Table 3.4

1990 Estimated Undercount Rates and Standard Errors Based on the Post-Enumeration Survey

State	Census	Original PES			Revised PES		
		Estimate	UC Rt.	SE	Estimate	UC Rt.	SE
California	29,760,021	30,888,075	3.652%	0.420%	30,594,537	2.728%	0.379%
U.S. total	248,709,873	253,979,140	2.075%	0.182%	252,712,822	1.584%	0.191%

SOURCE: "State Level Estimates and Estimated Undercount Rates, July 1992," Robinson, personal communication.

NOTES: UC Rt. = Undercount Rate

SE = Standard Error

PES = Post Enumeration Survey

A second condition assumes that California's undercount rate in 1990 was at least as high as the undercount rate in 1980. National estimates of the net undercount suggest an increase in the net undercount rate between 1980 and 1990 (Robinson, Ahmed, Das Gupta, and Woodrow, 1991; Robinson and Ahmed, 1992). California experienced rapid population growth during the decade, with a significant increase resulting from immigration. The very rapid growth rate in populations that are probably more difficult to enumerate (African Americans, Latinos, and Asians accounted for at least 75 percent of the state's total population growth during the decade) also suggests that the net undercount rate in 1990 was as high or higher than the 1980 net undercount rate. Accepting this condition (in addition to the assumption of a positive net undercount in both censuses) reduces the plausible range of total population change to between 6.2 million and 7.3 million.

Finally, the 1980 census and the 1990 census had similar content, and both included extensive outreach efforts. National estimates of the net undercount rate from the Post Enumeration Program (PEP) in 1980

(1.2 percent) and the PES in 1990 (1.6 percent revised) suggest an increase in the net undercount rate of one-third. The Robinson and Ahmed (1992) synthetic estimates suggest an increase of almost 60 percent in the net undercount rate between 1980 and 1990. Given the similarity between censuses and the ratios of the national net undercount rates for 1990 versus 1980, a third condition constrains net undercount rates for California in 1990 to be no more than 100 percent higher than net undercount rates in 1980. This condition further limits the range of total population change for the state to between 6.2 million and 6.9 million.

The subsequent analyses of the components of population change consider three undercount scenarios. The first assumes no undercount in either census, and is included to provide estimates consistent with census tabulations. The second assumes an increase in the net undercount rate from 3.0 percent in 1980 to 3.7 percent in 1990, representing a moderate increase in the absolute undercount of about 400,000 persons. For the purposes of this analysis, it is the absolute increase in the net undercount rather than the undercount rates themselves that are of importance. Thus, any combination of net undercount rates that produces an increase in the absolute undercount of 400,000 persons (for example, 1.5 percent in 1980 and 2.5 percent in 1990) will lead to essentially the same results in estimating population change. Given the empirical findings regarding undercount rates in the nation and in California, this scenario probably provides the most reasonable estimate of total population change for the decade. The third scenario represents a dramatic increase in net undercount rates and an increase of 800,000 in the absolute net undercount between 1980 and 1990. This upper bound implies a doubling of the undercount rate from 2.25 percent in 1980 to a very high 4.5 percent undercount rate in 1990. As mentioned previously, this upper bound is significantly higher than the highest empirical estimates of the 1990 net undercount rate, and is treated here as an extreme case.

Annual Population Change, 1980–1993

Annual estimates of the state's population are developed by both the Bureau of the Census and the California Department of Finance (see Table 3.5). Prior to 1989, the statewide estimates produced by the Department of Finance (DOF) and the Census Bureau were identical (differences in estimates prior to 1989 shown in Table 3.5 are a consequence of post-census revisions). Since 1989, the two sets of estimates have diverged as a result of methodological differences. The Census Bureau and DOF estimates include assumptions about undocumented immigration, however, and are not independent measures of population change according to this study's methodological approach.

Independent estimates of intercensal populations can be constructed through the use of various indicators of population size. These indicators include residential building permits, total occupied housing units (based on residential electrical customers), total housing units, driver licenses, school enrollment, births, deaths, Medicare enrollment, payroll employment, and labor force estimates. The censal ratio method can be used to develop population estimates based on combinations of the above administrative records. Table 3.6 and Figure 3.1 compare annual population estimates derived from three independent estimators with Census Bureau and DOF estimates (a fourth estimate is the average of the three independent estimates). Appendix A includes additional

17

Table 3.5

Estimates of California Population
(in thousands)

July 1	U.S. Census Bureau[a]	DOF[b]
1980	23,801	23,782
1981	24,286	24,278
1982	24,820	24,805
1983	25,360	25,336
1984	25,844	25,816
1985	26,441	26,402
1986	27,102	27,052
1987	27,777	27,717
1988	28,464	28,393
1989	29,218	29,142
1990	29,904	29,944
1991	30,416	30,565
1992	30,914	31,188
1993	31,220	31,517

[a]1980–1990 estimates: Edwin R. Byerly (1993). "State Population Estimates by Age and Sex: 1980 to 1992," U.S. Bureau of the Census, *Current Population Reports,* P25-1106, U.S. Government Printing Office, Washington, D.C.

1990 forward: "State Population Estimates and Components of Change 1990–1995," consistent with Department of Commerce Press Release CB96-10, issued 1/26/96, Population Distribution Branch, U.S. Bureau of the Census. Methodology may be found in *Current Population Reports,* P25-1127.

[b]California Department of Finance, *Estimates of the Population of the State of California with Components of Change and Crude Rates, 1941–1995,* Report 95 E-7. Sacramento, California, May 1996.

estimates and a discussion of the development of the independent population estimates.

While the total population estimates are similar (Figure 3.1), the annual population change implied by each of the estimators shows large

Table 3.6

California Population Estimates with No Undercount Adjustment
(in thousands)

April to April Change	Annual Population Change					
	Series A	Series B	Series C	Series D	Series E	Series F
1980–81	448	479	526	481	486	497
1981–82	378	436	415	437	519	522
1982–83	474	383	343	449	530	539
1983–84	457	459	440	464	493	498
1984–85	502	589	579	559	560	569
1985–86	700	696	704	704	634	645
1986–87	825	727	764	707	661	671
1987–88	777	740	801	749	673	684
1988–89	737	757	764	666	731	737
1989–90	793	825	757	876	805	730
1990–91	662	703	518	679	725	530
1991–92	468	540	349	484	658	502
1992–93	166	274	262	194	493	354
1980–1990	6,092	6,092	6,092	6,092	6,092	6,092
1990–1993	1,295	1,517	1,129	1,357	1,876	1,385
1980–1993	7,388	7,609	7,221	7,449	7,968	7,478
	April 1 Estimate					
1980	23,668	23,668	23,668	23,668	23,668	23,668
1981	24,116	24,147	24,194	24,148	24,154	24,165
1982	24,495	24,583	24,608	24,585	24,673	24,686
1983	24,969	24,966	24,952	25,035	25,203	25,225
1984	25,425	25,425	25,391	25,499	25,696	25,723
1985	25,927	26,014	25,970	26,058	26,256	26,292
1986	26,627	26,710	26,674	26,762	26,890	26,937
1987	27,453	27,437	27,438	27,469	27,551	27,608
1988	28,230	28,177	28,239	28,217	28,224	28,292
1989	28,967	28,935	29,003	28,884	28,955	29,030
1990	29,760	29,760	29,760	29,760	29,760	29,760
1991	30,422	30,463	30,277	30,439	30,485	30,288
1992	30,890	31,003	30,627	30,923	31,143	30,790
1993	31,055	31,277	30,889	31,117	31,636	31,144

SOURCES: **Series A:** Population estimate based on ratios of births for persons aged 0–4, school enrollment for persons aged 5–17, licensed drivers for persons aged 18–64, and Medicare enrollment ratio for persons aged 65+. **Series B:** Population estimate based on ratios of births for persons aged 0–4, school enrollment for persons aged 5–17, occupied households for persons aged 18–64, and Medicare enrollment ratio for persons aged 65+. **Series C:** Population estimate based on persons per occupied household, number of occupied households, and persons in group quarters. **Series D:** Average of three independent estimates (Series A, Series B, and Series C). **Series E:** California Department of Finance estimates, interpolated to April 1. **Series F:** U.S. Census Bureau population estimates, interpolated to April 1.

NOTE: See Appendix A for a discussion of the development of independent population estimates.

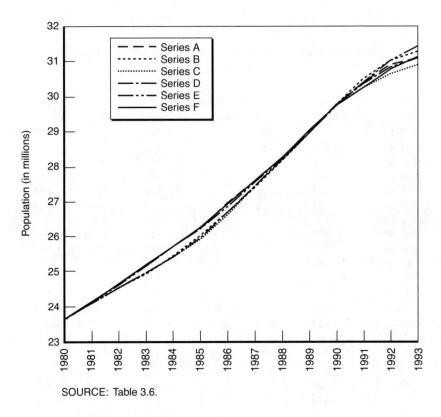

Population (in millions)

Series A
Series B
Series C
Series D
Series E
Series F

SOURCE: Table 3.6.

Figure 3.1—California Population Estimates, 1980–1993

differences (Figure 3.2). The accuracy of each estimate depends on the strength of the correlation between the estimator and actual population size. In particular, the accuracy of the final residual estimates of undocumented immigration will also depend on the estimator's ability to capture changes in the undocumented immigrant population of the state.[3]

---

[3] Of course, such errors could be partially offset or exacerbated by errors in estimates of the other components of population change.

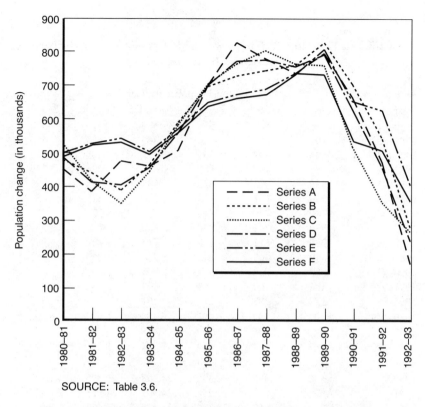

Population change (in thousands)

Series A
Series B
Series C
Series D
Series E
Series F

SOURCE: Table 3.6.

**Figure 3.2—Estimates of Annual Population Change in California,
1980–1993**

Adding adjustments for the net undercount will not change the
patterns observed in Figure 3.2, since the assumptions about undercount
rate adjustments are applied uniformly to each of the estimated
population series. The estimates shown here assume an undercount rate
adjustment that is a function of total population size, with intercensal
estimates adjusted for census undercounts on the basis of estimated
intercensal populations. Table 3.7 shows total population and annual
change estimates based on the middle series undercount scenario.

Table 3.7

California Population Estimates with a Moderate Increase in the Net Undercount (in thousands)

April to April Change	Annual Population Change					
	Series A	Series B	Series C	Series D	Series E	Series F
1980–81	475	507	557	509	515	526
1981–82	401	462	440	463	550	553
1982–83	503	407	364	477	563	572
1983–84	485	488	467	493	524	529
1984–85	533	626	616	595	595	605
1985–86	746	741	750	750	675	687
1986–87	880	776	814	754	705	716
1987–88	830	791	856	800	719	731
1988–89	789	811	818	713	782	789
1989–90	850	885	812	939	863	783
1990–91	687	730	537	705	753	548
1991–92	486	560	363	502	683	521
1992–93	172	285	277	201	511	367
1980–1990	6,492	6,492	6,492	6,492	6,492	6,492
1990–1993	1,345	1,574	1,172	1,409	1,947	1,436
1980–1993	7,837	8,067	7,664	7,901	8,439	7,928
	April 1 Estimate					
1980	24,398	24,398	24,398	24,398	24,398	24,398
1981	24,873	24,905	24,955	24,907	24,913	24,924
1982	25,274	25,367	25,394	25,370	25,463	25,477
1983	25,777	25,774	25,758	25,846	26,026	26,049
1984	26,262	26,261	26,225	26,340	26,549	26,578
1985	26,795	26,887	26,841	26,934	27,144	27,183
1986	27,540	27,628	27,591	27,684	27,820	27,870
1987	28,421	28,404	28,405	28,438	28,525	28,587
1988	29,251	29,195	29,261	29,238	29,245	29,318
1989	30,040	30,005	30,078	29,951	30,027	30,107
1990	30,890	30,890	30,890	30,890	30,890	30,890
1991	31,577	31,620	31,427	31,595	31,643	31,438
1992	32,063	32,180	31,790	32,098	32,326	31,959
1993	32,235	32,464	32,061	32,299	32,837	32,326

SOURCES: **Series A:** Population estimate based on ratios of births for persons aged 0–4, school enrollment for persons aged 5–17, licensed drivers for persons aged 18–64, and Medicare enrollment ratio for persons aged 65+. **Series B:** Population estimate based on ratios of births for persons aged 0–4, school enrollment for persons aged 5–17, occupied households for persons aged 18–64, and Medicare enrollment ratio for persons aged 65+. **Series C:** Population estimate based on persons per occupied household, number of occupied households, and persons in group quarters. **Series D:** Average of three independent estimates (Series A, Series B, and Series C). **Series E:** California Department of Finance estimates, interpolated to April 1. **Series F:** U.S. Census Bureau population estimates, interpolated to April 1.

NOTE: See Appendix A for a discussion of the development of independent population estimates.

Other undercount adjustment *methods* produce very similar total population and population change estimates. Since most of the estimated population growth in California occurred in the latter part of the 1980s, any undercount allocation that considers population will result in greater adjustments to estimates in the latter part of the 1980s. But even a crude linear extrapolation of undercount rate adjustments (that is, taking the undercount adjustment as a linear function of time) results in total population estimates and annual population change estimates that are very similar to those shown in Table 3.7.

In this study's residual components-of-change methodology, estimates of annual population change are an integral determinant of the final estimates of net undocumented immigration. For any given year, most of the annual uncertainty in the net undocumented immigration estimates originates with uncertainty regarding annual population change. Over the entire time span of the undocumented immigration estimates, most of the uncertainty in the total level of undocumented immigration is due to uncertainty about the undercount and thus population change.

4. Births and Deaths

Births and deaths are the most accurately recorded components of population change. Tabulations of births and deaths were developed from the California Department of Health Services data on vital events. Birth and death tabulations used here are based on place of residence rather than place of occurrence.

The registration of births and deaths is considered to be near universal in California (California Department of Health Services, 1993).[1] The number of unregistered births and deaths is almost certain to be so small as to be negligible, particularly in light of the potential magnitude of errors in estimates of the other components of population change. Any overregistration of births (for example, by foreign born

---

[1] The California Department of Health Services (DHS) reports that birth registration is considered to be complete for births that occur in California, and nearly so for out-of-state births to California residents. DHS cites a 1973 Census Bureau study which found birth registration to be 99.2 percent complete in the United States from 1964 through 1968. Death registration is considered to be "almost 100 percent" complete, with some underregistration of infant deaths, particularly those that occur in the first day of life.

nonresidents) should also be negligible, especially since the tabulations used here are based on place of residence.[2]

Since the birth and death tabulations are based on comprehensive recording of those events, adjustments for census undercounts will have no bearing on the birth and death estimates.

Natural increase rose steadily in the 1980s, fueled primarily by increasing numbers of births (see Table 4.1).

Table 4.1

Births, Deaths, and Natural Increase in California, 1980–1993
(in thousands)

April to April	Births	Deaths	Natural Increase
1980–81	407	188	219
1981–82	423	184	239
1982–83	431	188	243
1983–84	437	190	248
1984–85	452	202	251
1985–86	475	198	276
1986–87	487	205	282
1987–88	510	214	296
1988–89	540	217	323
1989–90	581	213	369
1990–91	610	211	399
1991–92	613	215	398
1992–93	595	216	379
1980–1990	4,743	1,998	2,745
1980–1993	6,561	2,641	3,920

SOURCE: Author's tabulations from California Department of Health Services data.

---

[2]Even this distinction between place of residence and place of occurrence is not particularly important. In 1991, for example, California residents had 609,228 live births, while a total of 610,393 live births occurred in the state (California Department of Health Services, 1993).

5. Total Net Migration

Total net migration for the decade is simply the difference between total population change and natural increase. Various estimates of total population change less natural increase will produce a range of estimates of total net migration. Because coverage for natural increase is taken as universal, any absolute increase in the net undercount between the 1980 and 1990 censuses results in an equivalent absolute increase in the estimate of net migration (see Table 5.1). Indeed, components-of-change measures based on complete counts of births and deaths and incomplete population counts will produce estimates of net migration that are too low.

Annual estimates of net migration depend on which series of population estimates is used. In general, the population estimates developed here as well as those of the Census Bureau and the California Department of Finance suggest high levels of net migration to California during the 1980s, with especially strong flows into the state in the late 1980s. Even with no adjustment for the undercount, annual net

Table 5.1

Estimates of Total Net Migration to California, 1980 to 1990
(in thousands)

Undercount Estimate	Total Population Change	Natural Increase	Net Migration
No undercount	6,092	2,745	3,347
1% in 1980 and 1990	6,154	2,745	3,409
3% in 1980, 3.7% in 1990	6,488	2,745	3,743
2.25% in 1980, 4.5% in 1990	6,950	2,745	4,205

increases in the state's population resulting from migration amounted to over 300,000 per year between 1985 and 1990 (Figure 5.1). A dramatic and unprecedented reversal in migration flows occurred beginning in 1990, and by 1993 all but one of the population estimates series suggest that California experienced net migration losses.

Net migration estimates adjusted for the undercount show the same general trends, but at higher levels, especially during the 1980s (Figure 5.2). Because undercount rate adjustments were held constant at 1990 levels for the post-1990 population estimates, net migration estimates for 1990–1993 that consider the undercount are not appreciably different from those shown in Figure 5.1.

The components of net migration estimated here and discussed below are net legal immigration, net domestic migration, and net undocumented immigration. Since legal immigration is relatively well recorded, the estimates of undocumented immigration depend heavily on accurate estimates of domestic net migration.

Net Legal Immigration

Estimates of legal immigration to California were obtained from the California Department of Finance. Department of Finance estimates are

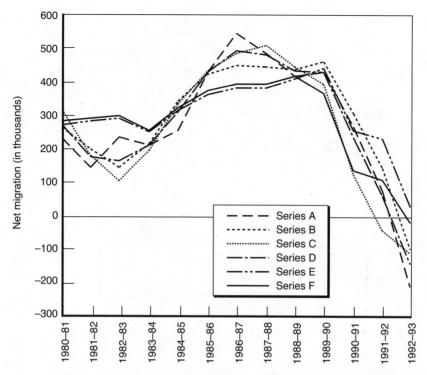

NOTE: See Table 3.6 for definition of the underlying population change series.

Figure 5.1—Total Annual Net Migration to California Under Alternative Population Change Scenarios, 1980–1993

based on intended state of residence and are derived from Immigration and Naturalization Service (INS) tapes as well as refugee data.[1] Persons granted amnesty under the provisions of the Immigration Reform and Control Act of 1986 (IRCA) are not included in the annual legal

---

[1] From INS tapes, we developed our own tabulations of legal immigrants admitted to the United States with California as the intended state of residence. The numbers developed were within a few thousand of the DOF tabulations, except for the final two years. The difference in the final years can be attributed to the inclusion of refugees at time of arrival in the DOF tabulations. The INS tapes do not include refugees until they obtain legal permanent resident status.

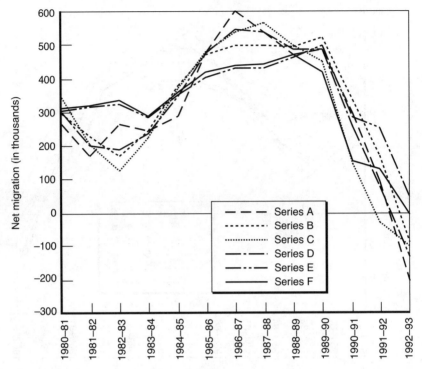

NOTE: See Table 3.6 for definition of the underlying population change series.

**Figure 5.2—Total Annual Net Migration to California, 1980–1993,
Adjusted for a Moderate Undercount Increase**

immigration estimates developed by DOF. As discussed later in this chapter, we have added some persons granted amnesty under the Special Agricultural Worker provisions of IRCA to the DOF estimates of legal immigration.[2] Total legal immigration to California and the United

---

[2] The Immigration Reform and Control Act of 1986 provides amnesty to formerly undocumented immigrants through two major programs: (1) the general legalization program, and (2) the Special Agricultural Worker (SAW) program. Persons granted amnesty under the general legalization program of IRCA (termed LAWs) were required to have lived continuously in the United States since January 1, 1982. In estimating annual components of population change, the adjustment of an individual's status from

States is thought to be well recorded, though emigration is very uncertain.[3] Estimates of legal immigration developed by the California Department of Finance from Immigration and Naturalization Service data suggest total foreign legal immigration from April 1, 1980 to April 1, 1990 was 1,632,500, and legal immigration between 1990 and 1993 was 646,000. Our adjustment for SAWs adds 74,000 to the estimate of legal immigration during the 1980s.

Alternative estimates of emigration will produce a range of estimates of net foreign migration. Unfortunately, estimates of emigration are somewhat speculative. Using period-of-immigration data from the 1980 and 1990 censuses for the United States, Ahmed and Robinson have estimated annual emigration of the foreign born at 195,000 per year during the 1980s, a substantial increase over the emigration estimate of 133,000 previously used by the Bureau of the Census in its population estimates and projections (Ahmed and Robinson, 1994). The methodology employed by Ahmed and Robinson produces emigration rates of zero or less for many countries of birth (including Mexico). The authors attribute these impossible rates to increased census coverage for foreign-born persons from those countries. Emigration rates of persons born in those countries are therefore estimated based on emigration rates of other foreign-born persons.

---

undocumented to legal resident should not be tabulated as a newly arrived legal immigrant. In California, almost one million persons applied for amnesty under the general provisions of IRCA, consistent with Passel and Woodrow's (1984) estimate that the 1980 census included just over one million undocumented immigrants in California. Persons granted amnesty under the SAW provision of IRCA were required to have worked in agriculture at least 90 days between May 1985 and May 1986, and were not required to establish residency in the United States.

[3] Emigration in this context consists of the movement abroad of legal United States residents.

However, Ellis and Wright (1996) compare responses to census questions from the *period of immigration* question with the responses to the *location of residence five years ago* question and conclude that the period-of-immigration question overestimates recent migration flows. They conclude that the magnitude of the overestimate increased from the 1970s to the 1980s. Ellis and Wright argue that the difference between the period-of-immigration estimates of foreign migration and the five-years-ago estimates results from both circular migration as well as wording of the period-of-immigration question—"When did this person come to the United States to stay?"[4] For California, we find large differences between the period-of-immigration and five-years-ago estimates of foreign migration. For persons aged 5 and over in 1990, the total number of persons recorded living abroad five years ago is 20 percent lower than the number recorded immigrating to the United States in either the period 1985–1986 or 1987–1990 (1.49 million versus 1.77 million). If Ellis and Wright are correct, then constructing emigration rates based on the period-of-immigration response may overstate emigration rates. For example, some immigrants who correctly responded in the 1980 census that they immigrated in 1970–1974 might have also correctly responded in the 1990 census that they immigrated most recently between 1981–1982. This shift to a more recent period of immigration will lower the size of the earlier period-of-immigration cohort and will incorrectly increase emigration rates.

Prior to 1950, the U.S. government kept records on emigration. Based primarily on those historical records, the Social Security

---

[4]The instructions for the question state, "If the person has entered the United States (that is, the 50 states and the District of Columbia) more than once, fill the circle for the latest year he/she came to stay."

Administration uses an emigration rate of 30 percent of current immigration in its projections (Duleep, 1994). However, current emigration rates might be lower than historical rates partly because the country of origin mix of recent immigrants is more heavily comprised of countries with relatively lower economic opportunity (Duleep, 1994; Woodrow-Lafield, 1996a).[5] The higher proportions of post–1965 legal immigrants admitted through refugee and family reunification programs should also lead to lower emigration rates (Woodrow-Lafield, 1996a). The Census Bureau middle series population projections for the nation developed in 1992 assumed an emigration rate of 15 percent (Duleep, 1994). State population projections developed in 1996 by the Census Bureau assume total emigration (including emigration of both foreign-born persons and persons born in the United States) of 160,000 per year for all states combined (Day, 1996). The estimates used here, as shown in Table 5.2, assume emigration rates of 22.5 percent of legal immigration, a figure that is midway between the historical estimates and those used in the Census Bureau middle series projections. In Chapter 6, the impact of alternative levels of emigration on estimates of net undocumented immigration is discussed.

One of the key issues in the estimate of legal immigration is the treatment of Special Agricultural Workers granted amnesty under the provisions of IRCA. Legal immigration estimates depend partly on the determination of the number of SAWs who became residents of the state as a result of the Act. Alternatively, SAWs who continue to engage in short-term cyclical migration will not increase net legal immigration as

---

[5] Woodrow-Lafield also argues that historic emigration rates of one-third may have been inflated as a result of return migration of Europeans as Europe experienced rapid economic growth.

Table 5.2

Legal Immigration to California, 1980–1993
(in thousands)

April to April	Legal Immigration	Net Legal Immigration, Using 22.5% Emigration of Legal Immigration, plus SAWs Adjustment
1980–81	163	126
1981–82	171	132
1982–83	149	115
1983–84	138	107
1984–85	148	114
1985–86	162	125
1986–87	164	127
1987–88	174	172
1988–89	184	179
1989–90	183	141
1990–91	189	146
1991–92	215	167
1992–93	242	188
1980–1990	1,633	1,339
1990–1993	646	501
1980–1993	2,279	1,840

SOURCE: California Department of Finance and author's estimates.

NOTE: The adjustment for SAWs added 37,000 immigrants in 1987–1988 and 1988–1989.

measured here. In this approach to measuring immigration, any stay of short duration will net to zero over the course of a year and thus is not considered. SAWs who had already established residence in the United States should not be treated as newly arrived legal immigrants when they adjust their status from undocumented to legal resident. In California, over 500,000 SAWs have been granted legal residency.[6]

---

[6]This and other tabulations of SAWs were generated from the "Immigration Reform and Control Act (IRCA) of 1986: 1992 Legalization Summary Public Use Tape."

The application period for the SAW program was June 1, 1987 to November 30, 1988. Over 150,000 California SAWs granted legal residency reported their date of last entry to the United States as coinciding with the application period. We assume that those reporting an earlier date of entry had already established residency in the United States. Of the SAWs reporting a last date of entry during the application period, some may have established residency in California prior to their last date of entry, some may still be engaged in short-term seasonal migration and therefore have not established residency in the United States, and still others established semi-permanent or permanent residency in California at the time of their application for amnesty. It is this last group which should be treated as new legal immigrants for the purposes of this methodology (which attempts to measure components of change in the *resident* population of California). Unfortunately, we have no way to estimate the size of this group. Complicating the estimates is the lack of reliability in the application data; Martin (1990a, p. 82) estimates that many of the SAW applications for amnesty were fraudulent, with "three to four times as many applicants as there would have been even if all California farmworkers employed in perishable commodities were illegal aliens." In the absence of a reliable basis to form an estimate, we arbitrarily estimate that half of the SAWs granted amnesty who reported a date of last entry from June 1982 through November 1988 were first-time permanent or semi-permanent resident settlers in California. In Chapter 6, we evaluate the sensitivity of the estimates of net undocumented immigration to alternative assumptions regarding SAWs.

Net Domestic Migration

With natural increase and legal migration relatively well known, the final residual estimates of undocumented migration will depend to a large extent on the estimates of domestic migration.

Tracking the movement of persons from one state to another is an uncertain undertaking. The United States has no restrictions on internal migration. Persons who move from one state to another are not required to register that movement. Surveys, censuses, and administrative records do not capture the entire resident population of the state, and movers are probably more likely to be missed by such records than are nonmovers. Nevertheless, numerous data sets do exist that give indications of interstate migration. Table 5.3 summarizes the data sets considered in this report.

The amount of information contained in the data sets varies considerably. The 1990 census has the advantage of covering the entire population (minus the undercount), but only records moves that occurred from April 1, 1985 to April 1, 1990. The Internal Revenue Service (IRS) and Department of Motor Vehicle (DMV) data can be used to develop annual estimates of domestic migration, but the data sets cover only specific subsets of the population. Another source of data, the March supplements of the Current Population Survey (CPS), can be used to develop annual estimates of the number of domestic migrants. The CPS is timely and provides detailed information, but suffers from imprecision because of small sample size. The CPS also has weighting problems across time and for state-level estimates.

Separate discussions of the estimates produced by each of the data sources follow. The chapter concludes with a comparison and evaluation of the estimates produced by these data sets.

Table 5.3

Sources of Estimates of Domestic Migration

Source	Basis of Determination of Migration Status	Coverage	Detail
1990 Census	Census question on location of residence five years prior to the census (April 1, 1985).	All persons completing the long form census questionnaire (about 1 in 6 households), weighted to reflect the entire population counted in the census.	Socioeconomic, demographic, and geographic characteristics; gross flows.
Current Population Survey	Survey question on location of residence one year prior to the survey (March of each year; five years earlier for the CPS in 1985).	Persons surveyed, weighted to reflect the total civilian population, excluding persons in institutions.	Socioeconomic, demographic, and geographic characteristics; gross flows.
Internal Revenue Service	Matching of income tax returns.	Persons and their dependents who file income tax returns in two consecutive years.	Geographic characteristics (by state); gross flows.
California Department of Motor Vehicles	Driver license interstate address changes (accumulated on a monthly basis).	Persons who move across state borders and who return the driver license of their prior state of residence.	Age and geographic characteristics; gross flows.

SOURCE: Johnson and Lovelady (1995).

Estimates Based on Driver License Address Changes

The California Department of Motor Vehicles produces an annual report that includes information on interstate driver license address changes. For interstate moves *to* California, the DMV tabulates the number of persons obtaining a driver license in California who were previously licensed in another state. Interstate moves *from* California are recorded when motor vehicle departments in other states return licenses of persons previously licensed in California who have obtained a new license in that other state.

Prior to 1993, the driver license address change data were tabulated and published by the California Department of Finance. The DOF monitored the data monthly, and sometimes made adjustments to the series based on inconsistencies in the reporting of California driver licenses received from other states. For fiscal year 1987, no driver license address change data are available. In that year, DMV field offices were automated, and temporary coding errors and inconsistencies in the data prevented the DOF from developing meaningful tabulations (California Department of Finance, 1992). Table 5.4 provides unadjusted interstate driver license address changes.

Potential problems with the driver license address change data fall into two categories: problems associated with the process and reporting of driver license address changes, and coverage issues. Problems associated with the processing and reporting of driver licenses include:

- Failure on the part of the applicant to report the possession of a driver license from another state.

- Failure of an interstate mover to obtain a new license in his/her new state of residence.

Table 5.4

Estimates of Domestic Migration for California: Unadjusted
Driver License Address Change Data
(in thousands)

Year (July to July)	Domestic In	Domestic Out	Net Domestic
1980–81	289	276	13
1981–82	260	258	2
1982–83	249	238	11
1983–84	254	245	10
1984–85	297	255	42
1985–86	323	246	77
1986–87	295	220	75
1987–88	n/a	n/a	n/a
1988–89	437	299	138
1989–90	430	345	85
1990–91	376	341	35
1991–92	342	353	(12)
1992–93	289	393	(104)
1993–94	274	396	(122)
Total 1980–1985	1,349	1,272	77
Total 1985–1990	1,485	1,110	375
Total 1980–1990	2,834	2,382	452

SOURCE: California Department of Finance and California Department of Motor Vehicles.

NOTE: The above data reflect revisions of out-migration flows to certain states.

- A lag between the time of the move and the time of reporting of the move to the DMV.[7]

---

[7]A 1974 field survey conducted for the Population Research Unit at the Department of Finance found that within a year after a move, 85 percent of drivers had reported their correct address to the DMV. Younger drivers were less likely to report changes than older drivers, and very recent movers were less likely to report changes than persons who had moved some time ago (Rasmussen, 1974). It is possible, perhaps probable, that accurate reporting of address changes to DMV has declined since this survey.

- A lack of diligence in reporting or collecting licenses of California out-migrants by motor vehicle departments in other states.

- A lack of diligence in reporting or collecting licenses of California in-migrants by motor vehicle field offices in California.

Such problems could severely affect the quality of the data.

Other potential problems with the driver license address change data include coverage issues. Many domestic migrants do not drive, particularly those over the age of 65 and obviously those under the age of 16. Some domestic migrants will stop driving around the time of the move, and will no longer need a driver license. And still others will not begin driving until just after the move, and therefore will not have a license from the prior state of residence. Such coverage issues can be partially resolved by making assumptions about the rate of noncoverage.

It is possible to examine coverage rates by comparing licensed drivers with population estimates. As shown in Table 5.5, the number of licensed drivers as a percentage of the estimated population exceeds 90 percent for all persons between the ages of 18 and 64. By five-year age group, only for persons aged 80 and over do coverage rates fall below 50 percent. Such high coverage rates provide confidence that the movement of persons between the ages of 18 and 64 can be captured by driver license address changes.

In using driver license address changes to estimate domestic migration for persons of all ages, the simplest method assumes that the migration patterns of licensed drivers are the same as those without driver licenses. Total interstate migration to/from California can then be estimated by applying the ratio of persons to licenses to the unadjusted

Table 5.5

California Licensed Drivers as a Percent of Total Population by Age Group

Age	1980			1990		
	Licenses	Population	Licensed Drivers Percent of Population	Licenses	Population	Licensed Drivers Percent of Population
18–19	716,424	896,274	80%	602,200	923,670	65%
20–24	2,082,334	2,355,965	88%	2,074,700	2,533,616	82%
25–29	2,140,776	2,232,964	96%	2,631,982	2,858,857	92%
30–34	1,937,550	2,010,051	96%	2,665,130	2,820,910	94%
35–39	1,486,511	1,552,444	96%	2,369,506	2,478,553	96%
40–44	1,179,340	1,262,494	93%	2,044,903	2,124,944	96%
45–49	1,065,752	1,164,134	92%	1,527,563	1,599,550	95%
50–54	1,062,704	1,195,800	89%	1,185,789	1,272,332	93%
55–59	1,054,344	1,202,140	88%	1,030,581	1,127,859	91%
60–64	837,950	992,428	84%	966,404	1,097,758	88%
65–69	647,887	839,247	77%	890,583	1,048,177	85%
70–74	434,190	631,731	69%	630,692	798,762	79%
75–79	246,449	448,406	55%	403,611	598,695	67%
80–84	105,936	276,849	38%	196,907	374,000	53%
85+	32,656	218,017	15%	74,165	292,217	25%
Total 18–64	13,563,684	14,864,694	91%	17,098,760	18,838,049	91%
Total 18+	15,030,802	17,278,944	87%	19,294,718	21,949,900	88%

SOURCE: Population Estimates Branch, Bureau of the Census; consistent with and described in *Current Population Reports*, Series P25-1106, and California Department of Motor Vehicles.

NOTE: Number of drivers estimated as of April 1 each year by linear interpolation.

driver license address changes. The implicit assumption in applying this ratio to interstate driver license address changes is that the ratio of persons per driver license address change is the same for domestic migrants as it is for nonmovers in the state. Such an assumption is weak, if for no other reason than that migration probabilities are known to vary with age.

An alternative approach, used in this report, is to use the 1990 census to estimate the age pattern of migration. Adjustments to the DLAC data were made based on persons per driver license for those aged 18 to 64 times movers of all ages per movers aged 18 to 64:

$$\text{DLAC}_{adj,x} = (P_{18\text{-}64,x}/L_{18\text{-}64,x})(M/M_{18\text{-}64})\,(\text{DLAC}_{unadj\ 18\text{-}64,\ x})$$

where $\text{DLAC}_{adj,x}$ = DLAC adjusted domestic migration estimate for year x

$P_{18\text{-}64,x}$ = population aged 18–64 in year x

$L_{18\text{-}64,x}$ = licensed drivers aged 18–64

M = domestic migrants of all ages based on census data (Public Use Microdata Sample)

$M_{18\text{-}64}$ = domestic migrants age adjusted 18–64 based on census data

and $\text{DLAC}_{unadj\ 18\text{-}64,\ x}$ = interstate driver license address changes for persons aged 18–64.

Adjustments were determined separately for in-migrants and out-migrants. The ratio of persons aged 18 to 64 to drivers aged 18 to 64 changed very little between 1980 and 1990, from 1.095 to 1.103 (based on U.S. Census Bureau revised age estimates for the 1980 and 1990 censuses). The 1990 Census Public Use Microdata Sample (PUMS) was used to estimate the ratio of domestic migrants of all ages to domestic migrants aged 18 to 64. Using the five-years-ago question, an estimated age at time of migration was developed (taking into account return/cyclical migration) for both domestic in-migrants and domestic out-migrants.[8] The PUMS tabulations adjusted to reflect time at age of migration produce ratio estimates of 1.35 for domestic in-migrants and 1.39 for domestic out-migrants. In other words, for every 100 domestic in-migrants aged 18 to 64, we estimate domestic in-migration of 135 for persons of all ages. Similarly, for every 100 domestic out-migrants aged 18 to 64, we estimate domestic out-migration of 139 for persons of all ages. The slightly higher ratio of out-migrants is consistent with 1985 CPS data, and with tax return data that show more exemptions per return for out-migrants.

---

[8]To adjust census data on movers to reflect age at time of move, domestic migrants were tabulated by individual year of age at the time of the April 1, 1990 census. Gross flow comparisons between census five-years-ago estimates and summed annual estimates of migration from other sources suggest that individual year data include many persons who will subsequently move within a few years. Only the recent return/cyclical migrants (actually, those who have not completed the return) will be represented in the census tabulations of domestic migrants. Equivalently, and perhaps more clearly, the census does not include cyclical domestic migrants who have completed the cycle, and these migrants are those who came early in the period. DLAC data, for example, do include those migrants. Assuming constant migration across the five years is a misallocation to the extent that eventual return migrants are still in the state on April 1, 1990, but completed return migrants are not. Assuming complete and accurate reporting in both the DLAC and census, the difference between the gross flows in the two series is the proportion of gross migrants who move in and out of the state within the period. This proportion is a function of the rate of return/continuing migration as well as the timing of those second moves; i.e., the proportion has both level and temporal aspects. Essentially this is a life table measure, with failure representing a return move (and also mortality, in fact). In estimating age at time of move for census gross migrants, the distribution of moves across the five-year period must take into account this return migration factor. Also, return migration is probably a function of age (most important) and income, and perhaps education. Without empirical data, we do not attempt to model these covariates. Using comparisons of gross migration flows, we estimate the size of the return migration component. From this, we develop a distribution of moves concentrated toward the end of the five-year period (27 percent in 1989–1990, 21 percent in 1988–1989, 19 percent in 1987–1988, 17 percent in 1986–1987, and 16 percent in 1985–1986). The estimation of age at time of migration is straightforward once this distribution of moves is developed. Contact the author for further details.

Determination of domestic migration based on the DLAC data for individual years during the 1980s is partly a function of the intercensal population estimates, treatment of the missing year of data, and undercount adjustments. Because the DOF and Census Bureau intercensal estimates are in close agreement, estimates of domestic migration differ only minimally when those two series are used as a basis for adjusting the DLAC estimates. Other intercensal population estimates, discussed in Chapter 3, also produce domestic migration estimates similar to those shown in Table 5.6. Using the IRS tax return

Table 5.6

Annual Estimates of Domestic Migration for California Based on Driver License Address Changes
(No undercount adjustment)
(in thousands)

April to April	In	Out	Net
1980–81	437	422	15
1981–82	394	401	(7)
1982–83	372	372	(496)
1983–84	374	372	2
1984–85	423	387	36
1985–86	467	380	87
1986–87	445	346	100
1987–88	514	381	133
1988–89	619	442	177
1989–90	639	512	127
1990–91	579	526	52
1991–92	524	543	(19)
1992–93	455	597	(143)
1980–1985	2,000	1,954	46
1985–1990	2,685	2,061	624
1980–1990	4,685	4,015	670
1990–1993	1,558	1,666	(109)
1980–1993	6,243	5,682	561

SOURCE: Author's estimates. See text for methodology.

NOTE: Missing year, 1987–1988, interpolated. Adjustments applied to DOF population estimates.

patterns of change in gross flows to estimate the missing year of DLAC data results in an increase of almost 50,000 net migrants over a simple linear extrapolation of the DLAC data across the missing year.

The estimates are somewhat more sensitive to adjustments for the census undercounts. For example, a moderate increase in the state's net undercount rate leads to an increase in total population change of 400,000 and an increase of over 100,000 in the DLAC-based net domestic migration estimates when compared to estimates with no undercount adjustment. For domestic out-migrants, net undercount rates for the United States are perhaps a more appropriate adjustment, since out-migrants are by definition residents of other states at the time of the census. Use of U.S. net undercount rates (1.2 percent in 1980 and 1.6 percent in 1990) leads to an additional increase in the net domestic migration estimate for the decade of approximately 75,000.

Estimates Based on Internal Revenue Service Tax Return Data

The Internal Revenue Service estimates interstate migration flows of taxpayers by matching tax returns from year to year. Matching is based on the social security number of the primary taxpayer. If the state in the address on the most recent tax return is different from the state in the address of the previous year's return, then the taxpayer and the dependents on the return are considered interstate migrants; if the match indicates no change in state, then the taxpayer and the dependents are considered nonmigrants; and if no match can be made, the tax return is not considered. Table 5.7 provides unadjusted IRS estimates of interstate migration to and from California (U.S. Internal Revenue Service, 1995).

Table 5.7

Unadjusted Internal Revenue Service Interstate Migration Flows for California
(Based on exemptions)

Period	Domestic In	Domestic Out	Net	Nonmovers
1970–73	1,035,213	1,149,892	(114,679)	n/a
1973–74	n/a	n/a	n/a	n/a
1974–75	n/a	n/a	n/a	n/a
1975–76	491,091	461,821	29,270	n/a
1976–77	515,277	498,002	17,275	n/a
1977–78	n/a	n/a	n/a	n/a
1978–79	524,370	528,560	(4,190)	n/a
1979–80	n/a	n/a	n/a	n/a
1980–81	493,410	477,121	16,289	n/a
1981–82	492,599	447,438	45,161	n/a
1982–83	463,631	387,734	75,897	n/a
1983–84	480,914	428,013	52,901	n/a
1984–85	487,621	396,033	91,588	n/a
1985–86	492,657	401,984	90,673	20,154,469
1986–87	501,494	402,325	99,169	20,598,864
1987–88	471,035	408,690	62,345	20,276,697
1988–89	451,527	454,342	(2,815)	20,975,225
1989–90	446,309	520,362	(74,053)	22,510,549
1990–91	397,444	531,946	(134,502)	23,010,999
1991–92	372,254	542,349	(170,095)	23,340,798
1992–93	319,966	625,119	(305,153)	23,236,233

SOURCE: U.S. Internal Revenue Service (1995).

NOTE: Exemptions refer to exemptions in most recent filing year; for example, exemptions for 1984–1985 refer to exemptions reported for tax year 1984 (as of December 31, 1984) for moves that occurred between filing in 1984 (of 1983 taxes) and filing in 1985 (of 1984 taxes).

Potential problems with the data include:

- Lack of complete coverage—not everyone files a return or is listed as a dependent in two subsequent years. The migration patterns of persons who do not file in subsequent years might be very different from those who do.

- Changes in filing status from one year to the next will result in nonmatches. For example, an individual who moves out of his/her parents' home to a different state and files a tax return as a primary taxpayer will not be matched and will therefore not be considered an interstate migrant.

- Dependents might have moved or not moved independently of the primary taxpayer.

As shown in Figure 5.3 and Figure 5.4, census data suggest that the domestic migration flow out of California was more heavily comprised of persons at lower income levels than the domestic migration flow to the state. This suggests that the IRS-based estimates of domestic migration overstate domestic migration to the state, since it can be expected that lower-income households are less likely to file income taxes than higher-income households.

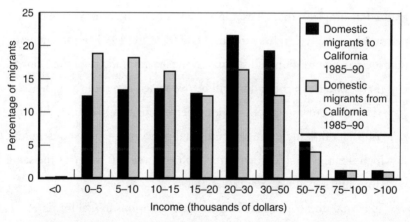

SOURCE: Author's tabulations from the 1990 census (5% Public Use Microdata Sample).

NOTE: Non-family households consist of persons living alone or in households with unrelated individuals; incomes are for 1989.

Figure 5.3—Distribution of Total Personal Income for Domestic Migrants to and from California in Non-Family Households

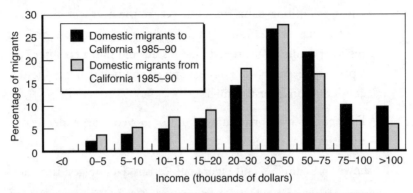

SOURCE: Tabulations from the 1990 census (5% Public Use Microdata Sample).

NOTE: Family households consist of persons living in households with related individuals; incomes are for 1989.

Figure 5.4—Distribution of Total Personal Income for Domestic Migrants to and from California in Family Households

We can also use 1990 census data to examine the IRS tax return method assumption that all exemptions in a household move when the person filing the return has moved. Data from the 1990 census suggest that such an assumption will slightly overstate domestic migration flows, and that domestic in-migration will be overstated at a slightly higher rate than domestic out-migration. Among persons in family households, the ratio of total domestic in-migrants to total persons in family households in which the householder moved to California was .96, whereas the same ratio for domestic out-migrants was .94.

The total number of matched return exemptions in California represents approximately three-fourths of the state's total population. Estimates of total domestic migration can be developed from IRS tax return data by applying an adjustment or weighting factor to individual year IRS data:[9]

$$\text{IRS}_{adj,x} = \text{IRS}_{unadj,x} (P_x / E_x)$$

where $\text{IRS}_{adj,x}$ = IRS tax return-based estimates of total domestic migration in year x

$\text{IRS}_{unadj,x}$ = total exemptions of interstate domestic migrants in year x

P_x = population in year x

and E_x = total exemptions for all tax filers.

These factors (that is, P_x/E_x) are lower than the adjustment factors used for the DMV data, and indicate that tax return data provide more complete coverage of the entire population than the driver license data. The undercoverage rate for the IRS data is about 24 percent, compared to an undercoverage rate of about 33 percent for the DMV data.[10]

Domestic net migration for the decade according to the adjusted tax return data totaled just over 600,000. The decennial estimates are not sensitive to which population series was used in the adjustment, but are higher when census undercounts are taken into consideration (see Table 5.8). In particular, the estimates of domestic net migration are substantially higher when United States undercount rates (instead of California undercount rates) are used to adjust out-migration estimates. Indeed, any differential adjustment of out- versus in-migration flows can

---

[9]Total exemptions are not available for years prior to 1985. The adjustment factor used in those years was that of the average 1985–1990 ratio of population to total exemptions.

[10]The total number of exemptions listed in matched returns for tax year 1990 in California was 23.0 million, compared to an estimated 19.3 million licensed drivers as of April 1, 1990.

Table 5.8

Estimates of Domestic Migration for California, 1980–1990, Based on IRS Tax Return Data
(in thousands)

Item	Domestic In	Domestic Out	Domestic Net
Unadjusted exemptions	4,781	4,324	457
Exemptions weighted to reflect DOF population estimates	6,309	5,705	604
Exemptions weighted to reflect Census Bureau population estimates	6,320	5,715	605
Exemptions weighted to reflect DOF population estimates adjusted for the undercount	6,526	5,902	624
Exemptions weighted to reflect DOF population estimates adjusted for California and U.S. undercount rates	6,526	5,788	738

NOTE: Undercount adjustment assumes undercount rates of 3.0 percent in 1980 and 3.7 percent in 1990 in California, and 1.2 percent in 1980 and 1.6 percent in 1990 for the United States.

lead to substantial differences in estimates of net migration, which will be directly reflected in estimates of net undocumented migration. Tables 5.9 and 5.10 provide annual estimates of domestic migration based on tax return data with alternative undercount scenarios.

Census and Current Population Survey Multiyear Estimates

Estimates of domestic migration from the 1990 census are based on responses to the mobility question asked of persons who completed the long-form census questionnaire. Specifically, the 1990 census asked one respondent from each household to answer the following question for each person in the household:

Table 5.9

Annual Estimates of Domestic Migration for California Based on IRS Tax Return Data with No Undercount Adjustment
(in thousands)

April to April	DOF Based Weighting Factor			Census Based Weighting Factor		
	In	Out	Net	In	Out	Net
1980–81	651	630	21	652	631	22
1981–82	650	590	60	651	591	60
1982–83	612	512	100	613	513	100
1983–84	635	565	70	636	566	70
1984–85	643	523	121	645	524	121
1985–86	640	522	118	641	523	118
1986–87	653	524	129	655	525	129
1987–88	639	555	85	641	556	85
1988–89	609	612	(4)	610	614	(4)
1989–90	577	673	(96)	577	673	(96)
1990–91	516	691	(175)	513	687	(174)
1991–92	488	710	(223)	482	702	(220)
1992–93	429	838	(409)	422	825	(403)
1980–1985	3,191	2,819	372	3,197	2,824	373
1985–1990	3,118	2,886	232	3,124	2,891	233
1980–1990	6,309	5,705	604	6,320	5,715	605
1990–1993	1,433	2,239	-806	1,417	2,214	(797)
1980–1993	7,742	7,944	-203	7,738	7,929	(191)

SOURCE: Author's estimates. See text for methodology.

Did this person live in this house or apartment 5 years ago (on April 1, 1985)?

If the response was "No," the respondent was instructed to write in the state or foreign country of residence five years ago. Tabulations of domestic in-migrants were derived from the 5 percent Public Use Microdata Sample for California, whereas tabulations of domestic out-migrants were derived from tabulations of the 5 percent Public Use Microdata Sample for the United States.

Table 5.10

Annual Estimates of Domestic Migration for California Based on IRS Tax Return Data with Undercount Adjustments
(in thousands)

April to April	Moderate Undercount Increase					High Undercount Increase				
	Domestic In	Domestic Out Based on U.S. Undercount Rate	Net	Domestic Out Based on California Undercount Rate	Net	Domestic In	Domestic Out Based on U.S. Undercount Rate	Net	Domestic Out Based on California Undercount Rate	Net
1980–81	672	637	34	649	22	667	637	30	645	22
1981–82	671	598	73	609	62	668	598	69	606	61
1982–83	632	518	113	528	103	630	518	111	526	103
1983–84	656	573	83	584	72	654	573	82	582	72
1984–85	665	530	135	540	125	665	530	135	540	125
1985–86	662	530	132	540	122	663	530	133	541	122
1986–87	676	532	144	543	134	678	532	146	544	134
1987–88	662	563	99	575	88	665	563	102	577	88
1988–89	631	622	9	635	(4)	635	622	13	639	(4)
1989–90	599	684	(85)	699	(99)	604	684	(80)	705	(100)
1990–91	536	702	(166)	717	(181)	541	702	(162)	724	(183)
1991–92	506	722	(216)	737	(231)	511	722	(211)	744	(233)
1992–93	445	851	(406)	869	(424)	449	851	(402)	877	(428)
1980–1985	3,295	2,857	438	2,911	384	3,283	2,857	427	2,900	383
1985–1990	3,231	2,931	300	2,991	240	3,246	2,931	315	3,006	240
1980–1990	6,526	5,788	738	5,902	624	6,529	5,788	742	5,906	623
1990–1993	1,487	2,275	(788)	2,324	(837)	1,500	2,275	(775)	2,345	(844)
1980–1993	8,013	8,063	(50)	8,226	(213)	8,030	8,063	(34)	8,251	(221)

NOTE: Adjustments applied to DOF population estimates. Moderate undercount increase: 3.0% in 1980, 3.7% in 1990. High undercount increase: 2.25 % in 1980, 4.5% in 1990.

The Current Population Survey is a monthly survey conducted by the Bureau of the Census for the Bureau of Labor Statistics. The data used in this report come from the March supplemental survey, also referred to as the Annual Demographic Survey. Surveyors asked one respondent from each household questions about each member of the household. The migration data were taken from responses to the question:

> Was . . . living in this house (apt.) 1 year ago; that is on March 1, 199x?

If the response was "No," the respondent was further questioned regarding the location of the prior place of residence. Persons living in California at the time of the survey and who lived in some other state one year earlier were tabulated as domestic in-migrants, whereas persons living outside of California at the time of the survey and who lived in California one year earlier were tabulated as domestic out-migrants. The 1985 CPS question was based on location of residence five years ago, whereas the CPS for other years asked location of residence one year ago.

The 1990 census and 1985 CPS five-years-ago questions cannot be used directly to estimate net domestic migration in the analysis of components framework. Adjustments must be made for domestic migrants not included in the universe. The universe includes only persons at least five years of age and still alive at the time of the census/survey. The impact of these omissions on the five-years-ago estimate of net undocumented migration is not especially problematic. We can estimate domestic net migration for these two groups. More problematic, as discussed below, are the small sample sizes and weighting problems of the CPS.

Combining the 1990 census estimates of net domestic migration (unadjusted) with the 1985 Current Population Survey estimates gives a decennial (1980–1990) estimate of net domestic migration to California of 519,000. Adjusting for persons under five (by assuming migration patterns of 0–4 year olds to be the same as for persons of other ages) increases the estimate to 542,000. Taking into account mortality (by using crude death rates) makes little difference, increasing the estimate to 552,000.

Current Population Survey Annual Estimates

Alternatively, the CPS one-year-ago questions from 1981 to 1994 can be used to estimate annual domestic migration. Annual estimates are not available for 1984–1985 (when a five-years-ago question was asked) nor are estimates of domestic out-migration available for 1980–1981.

Because of the small sample size, the CPS estimates are imprecise. Confidence intervals (90 percent) for the gross flows vary from year to year, but are generally ±120,000 around the point estimates. Net domestic migration estimates are even more imprecise, with 90 percent confidence intervals of about ±160,000 around the point estimates.[11]

Trends in the CPS estimates must be interpreted with caution because they are imprecise.[12] In general, the estimates show increasing

---

[11]For 1988–1989, a reduced 1989 CPS sample resulted in confidence intervals about one-third wider. See Johnson and Lovelady (1995) for a discussion of CPS confidence interval estimation.

[12]Changes in CPS weights over time also require that trends be interpreted with caution. In addition, the CPS weights are not controlled to independent state population estimates. The potential errors in the CPS-based estimates reported here caused by these weighting issues, however, pale in comparison with the imprecision resulting from the small sample sizes. The wide confidence intervals reflect the imprecision of the estimates resulting from small sample sizes.

levels of domestic out-migration and decreasing levels of domestic in-migration from the early 1980s to the early 1990s (see Table 5.11).

Comparison of the Domestic Migration Estimates

Because the data sources used to develop domestic migration estimates cover different segments of the population at different points in time with different means of identifying migrants, it is not surprising that the estimates developed from these various data sources contain substantial differences. In this components-of-change approach, these differences will be directly reflected in estimates of net undocumented immigration. This section explores these differences. First, we compare *annual* estimates of domestic migration developed from the CPS, DLAC,

Table 5.11

Estimates of Domestic Migration for California Based on Current Population Survey Data, Unadjusted

| | Sum of Weights (population) | | |
| | Domestic Migrants | | |
CPS Year	In	Out	Net
1982	573,747	611,393	−37,646
1983	566,944	496,718	70,226
1984	595,021	581,009	14,012
1986	637,139	572,412	64,727
1987	575,970	526,776	49,194
1988	513,263	574,626	−61,363
1989	611,015	747,993	−136,978
1990	652,266	650,394	1,872
1991	559,523	593,599	−34,076
1992	526,239	621,030	−94,791
1993	421,842	731,273	−309,431
1994	398,811	634,617	−235,806

SOURCE; Author's calculations from 1981–1994 Current Population Surveys.

and IRS tax return data. Second, estimates of domestic migration over multiyear time periods are contrasted.

By Single Year

The DLAC, IRS, and CPS based estimates are all based on single-year time frames. While the DLAC and IRS tax return based estimates of domestic *net* migration for the decade are not extremely different, estimates of domestic net migration by year are quite different as are estimates of the gross flows. The differences in the domestic net migration estimates (Figure 5.5) can be isolated and evaluated by examining gross flows. Figure 5.6 and Figure 5.7 compare domestic in-migration estimates and domestic out-migration estimates based on the IRS, DLAC, and CPS series.

Estimates of domestic in-migration differ sharply between the series. Prior to 1987–1988, the CPS and IRS tax return based estimates show much higher domestic migration flows into the state than the DLAC based estimates. The DLAC estimates even lie outside the wide 90-percent confidence interval of the CPS estimates. After 1987–1988, the estimates of domestic in-migration are similar, especially in terms of the trend.

Estimates of domestic out-migration are also much higher in the CPS and IRS tax return series than in the DLAC based series. In this case, the IRS tax return based estimates lie within the 90-percent confidence intervals of the CPS estimate for each year, whereas the DLAC based estimates fall outside the wide confidence intervals for many of the years prior to 1989–1990.

Our analysis suggests that the IRS based estimates are more accurate than the DLAC estimates. Between July 1987 and July 1988, the

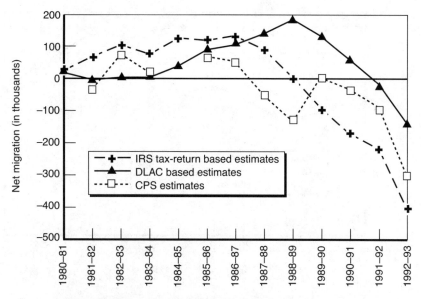

SOURCE: Author's estimates and tabulations.

NOTE: IRS tax return data and DMV driver license address change (DLAC) data have been adjusted to reflect total moves. The estimates do not include adjustments for the undercount.

Figure 5.5—Estimates of Annual Domestic Net Migration to California from Current Population Survey Data, IRS Tax Return Based Estimates, and Driver License Address Change (DLAC) Based Estimates

California Department of Motor Vehicles automated all its field offices in the state. The impact of this automation is apparent in Figure 5.8. Prior to 1987–1988, the estimates of domestic in-migration based on the DLAC data are consistently much lower than those based on the IRS data. After the automation, the reporting and recording of drivers moving to California from other states improved dramatically, so that the unadjusted DLAC estimates of domestic in-migrants are nearly as high as the IRS tax return estimates. The adjusted DLAC based estimates are slightly higher than but in close agreement with the IRS estimates. The

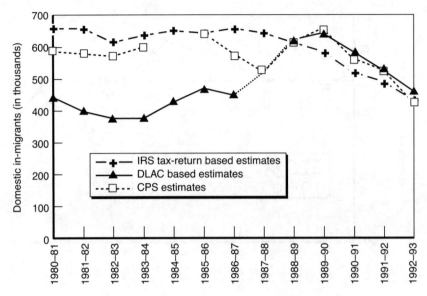

SOURCE: Author's estimates and tabulations.

NOTE: IRS tax return data and DMV driver license address change (DLAC) data have been adjusted to reflect total moves. The estimates do not include adjustments for the undercount.

Figure 5.6—Estimates of Annual Domestic In-Migration to California from Current Population Survey Data, IRS Tax Return Based Estimates, and Driver License Address Change (DLAC) Based Estimates

automation appears to have done little if anything to improve estimates of domestic out-migration. As shown in Figure 5.7, the trends in domestic out-migration are similar between the two series, but the DLAC based estimates remain substantially lower than the IRS tax return based estimates even after the automation. This is not surprising, since the DLAC estimates of domestic out-migration depend on the efficiency with which motor vehicle departments and offices *outside of California* return driver licenses to the California Department of Motor Vehicles headquarters in Sacramento. Automating California field offices did not affect this process.

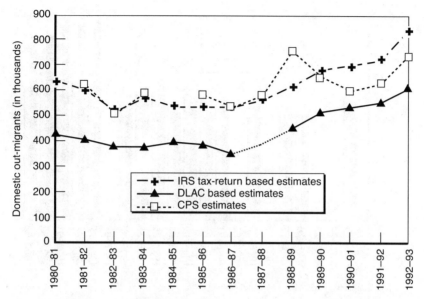

SOURCE: Author's estimates and tabulations.

NOTE: IRS tax return data and DMV driver license address change (DLAC) data have been adjusted to reflect total moves. The estimates do not include adjustments for the undercount. No DLAC data are available for 1987–88.

Figure 5.7—Estimates of Annual Domestic Out-Migration from California Based on Current Population Survey Data, IRS Tax Return Based Estimates, and Driver License Address Change (DLAC) Based Estimates

In addition, the IRS tax return based estimates consistently fall within the 90-percent confidence intervals of the imprecise CPS estimates, whereas the DLAC based estimates often fall outside these wide intervals. Multiyear comparisons, discussed below, reinforce these conclusions.

The consistency of the IRS tax return based estimates and the CPS estimates, coupled with the dramatic change in DLAC estimates of in-migration that accompanied the improvement in reporting, strongly

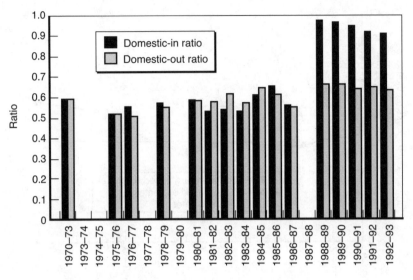

SOURCE: Author's calculations.

**Figure 5.8—Ratio of Unadjusted DLAC:IRS Domestic Migration
Flows for California**

suggest that the IRS tax return based estimates are the most reliable
annual series available.

Multiyear Period Comparisons

Because the 1990 census and 1985 CPS domestic migration
estimates are based on residence five years prior to the census/survey,
they are not directly comparable to the annual estimates produced by the
DLAC, IRS, and non-1985 CPS data series. Summing the annual
estimates derived from the IRS, DLAC, and CPS data will not produce
gross domestic flow estimates comparable to the five-years-ago estimates
from the 1990 census and 1985 CPS, but should produce similar
estimates of net migration. Even if there were no coverage differences
and domestic migration were perfectly recorded in each of the data sets,

the gross flows of domestic migration from the census and 1985 CPS would be lower than the five-year sums of the annual gross flows from the other estimates because of return migration. However, because such moves are self-canceling on a net flow basis, the net migration figures from the census should be similar to the five-year sum of the net migration figures from the estimates based on the other data series,[13] with some exceptions (see Table 5.12). It is important to remember that the migration scenarios in Table 5.12 probably represent only a small proportion of interstate and international migrations. The most common movements in the five-year period—all nonsequential moves, all multiple moves entirely within the United States, and all cyclical moves directly between California and abroad—would be tabulated (on a net basis) similarly by both the census and CPS measure.

Differences between the estimates of domestic migration from the four data sets are substantial. As shown in Table 5.13, gross flows both into and out of California are as expected much higher for the summed annual estimates (DLAC, CPS, and IRS) than for the five-year period estimates. In particular, the DLAC, CPS, and IRS domestic in-migration summed estimates for the five years 1985–1990 range from 28 percent to 50 percent higher than the 1990 census five-year period

---

[13]For example, a person who moves from California to Texas in 1986 and then returns to California in 1989 will not be counted as a domestic migrant in the 1990 census. In this example, the migrant's residence in both 1985 and 1990 was California. In the other data series, such a return migrant would appear as a domestic migrant from California in 1986 and a domestic migrant to California in 1989. Summing the gross annual flows over the five-year period would include the example migrant as both a domestic in-migrant and a domestic out-migrant. The effect of such return migration on the net migration five-year sum, however, would be zero (plus one domestic in-migrant in 1989 minus one domestic out-migrant in 1986). Thus, while annual estimates based on *gross* flows summed over the five-year period will exceed the census gross flows, the estimates of *net* migration should be similar.

Table 5.12

Migration Scenarios That Result in Different Net Migration Counts
(Annual measure versus census)

Scenario	Residence			California Net Migration Count	
	In 1985	In 1986–1989	In 1990	Per Census	Per Annual Measures
A	California	Abroad	California	0	+1 foreign
B	California	Other state	Abroad	0	−1 domestic
C	California	Abroad	Other state	−1 domestic	0
D	Other state	California	Abroad	0	+1 domestic
E	Other state	Abroad	California	+1 domestic	+1 foreign
F	Abroad	California	Abroad	0	+1 foreign
G	Abroad	California	Other state	0	−1 domestic
H	Abroad	Other state	California	+1 foreign	+1 domestic
I	Not born	California	Other state	0	−1 domestic
J	Not born	Other state	California	0	+1 domestic
K	Not born	Abroad	California	0	+1 foreign
L	California	Other state	Not alive	0	−1 domestic
M	Other state	California	Not alive	0	+1 domestic
N	Abroad	California	Not alive	0	+1 foreign

Table 5.13

Multiyear Comparisons of Domestic Migration for California

Item	1980–1985 In	Out	Net	1985–1990 In	Out	Net
1990 Census				2,090,910	1,893,024	197,885
1985 CPS	1,969,822	1,615,368	354,455			
DLAC adjusted, no undercount, missing year extrapolated	2,000,021	1,954,239	45,782	2,685,338	2,060,984	624,354
IRS adjusted, no undercount, intercensal weights based on Census Bureau estimates	3,196,523	2,823,972	372,552	3,123,849	2,891,204	232,645
CPS, single year questions				2,989,653	3,072,201	(82,548)

	1980–1984	1981–1984	1981–1984
CPS, single year questions	2,315,983	1,689,120	46,592

NOTE: 1990 Census and 1985 CPS have been adjusted for migration of persons aged 0–4 and deaths to migrants.

estimate. The 90-percent CPS confidence interval for the five-year summed domestic in-migration estimate includes both the DLAC and IRS tax return based estimates.

As expected, the domestic out-migration estimates for the 1985–1990 period are also much higher for the summed annual estimates compared to the 1990 census five-year period estimate. However, the DMV summed estimate for domestic out-migration is much lower than the CPS and IRS estimates. The 90-percent CPS confidence interval for domestic out-migration does not include the DLAC based estimate, but the IRS tax return based estimate is well within the confidence interval (see Table 5.14).

On a net basis, the IRS tax return based estimates are consistent with the census and CPS estimates. The DLAC based estimates are much higher than the other estimates for 1985–1990, and appear as a low outlier for the 1980–1985 period. In general, the CPS, IRS, and census estimates are consistent. In particular, as discussed earlier, the DLAC data differ from the other data sets primarily in estimates of domestic out-migrants. It is probable that persons leaving the state are not adequately captured by the DLAC data. At the same time, since the automation of DMV field offices, the California Department of Motor Vehicles appears to have become much more efficient at collecting out-

Table 5.14

90-Percent Confidence Intervals for Current Population Survey Estimates of Domestic Migration to and from California

	1985 Five Years Ago		Sum of 1985–1990	
	Low	High	Low	High
Domestic In	1,642,164	2,053,018	2,710,726	3,268,580
Domestic Out	1,329,006	1,701,258	2,786,103	3,358,297
Domestic Net	55,253	609,665	–482,111	317,017

of-state driver licenses than other states are at collecting and returning California driver licenses. Thus, estimates of domestic migration based on the DLAC data since the automation overstate net flows into the state.

Annual estimates of undocumented immigration depend on the choice of domestic migration estimates. Estimates of domestic migration from the DLAC data and the CPS point estimates are not reliable (with the possible exception of DLAC based domestic in-migration estimates after 1987–1988). The IRS tax return based domestic migration estimates are consistent with the census estimates, the CPS estimates, and the DLAC patterns (not levels) of domestic migration gross flows. Thus, the IRS tax return based estimates represent the most reliable series of annual domestic migration flows, and form the basis for the determination of undocumented immigration estimates.

6. Net Undocumented Immigration Estimates

In this methodological approach, net undocumented migration is the residual after accounting for all other components of population change. Given the previous components-of-change estimates, it is now possible to estimate net undocumented immigration.

Note that decennial estimates of net undocumented migration in this report and summations of the annual estimates of net undocumented migration cannot be used to directly determine estimates of the stock of undocumented immigrants. Simply adding the sum of net undocumented migration estimates to a 1980 estimate of the stock of undocumented immigrants will overcount the stock of undocumented immigrants primarily due to adjustments of undocumented immigrants to a legal status (through the amnesty provisions of the Immigration Reform and Control Act of 1986) and also due to mortality.

Over thirty series of annual net undocumented immigration estimates are developed. For each of the three undercount assumptions, six different estimates of annual population change are combined with two methods of estimating domestic migration to produce thirty-six different series of estimates of annual net undocumented immigration. Additional series are developed to evaluate the sensitivity of the estimates to other assumptions. Each series incorporates various assumptions about net domestic migration as well as annual population change.

Baseline estimates of net undocumented immigration between 1980 and 1993 are developed here from six population estimates (not adjusted for the undercount), vital records of births and deaths, estimates of net legal immigration, and net domestic migration estimates derived from IRS and DLAC data. Much of the annual variation in the undocumented immigration estimates is driven by underlying differences in the population estimates (see the discussion on pp. 76–78). The baseline series also includes two sets of domestic migration estimates, one based solely on IRS tax return data and a second incorporating some DLAC data (see pp. 80–82).

As shown in Figure 6.1, baseline estimates of net undocumented migration suggest a rapid increase in undocumented immigration in the last part of the 1980s and a strong downturn in the early 1990s (see also Table 6.1 and Table 6.2). Specifically, the estimates developed here indicate the following patterns of net undocumented immigration from 1980 through 1994:

- **1980 to 1985:** As shown in Figure 6.1, undocumented immigration to California occurred at a relatively low level during the early 1980s. Between 1980 and 1985, for example, the baseline estimates suggest that net undocumented immigration averaged less than 100,000 per year.

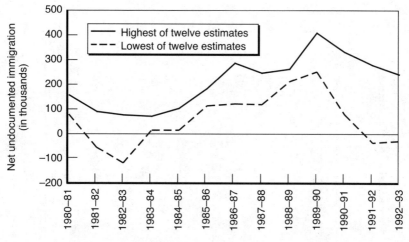

NOTE: Assumes no undercount adjustment.

Figure 6.1—Baseline Range of Net Undocumented Immigration
Estimates for California

- **1986 to 1989:** Net undocumented immigration rose
  throughout the middle of the 1980s, reaching a peak of well over
  200,000 between April 1989 and April 1990. Because these are
  net estimates this rise could be due to either fewer undocumented immigrants leaving the state, or an increase in the
  number of undocumented immigrants entering the state, or a
  combination of both factors.

- **Since 1990:** A sharp decline in net undocumented immigration
  to California has occurred since 1990, so that by 1992–1993,
  the net flow of undocumented immigrants to the state may have
  declined to less than 100,000 per year.

Although differences between the estimates for any one year are
large, each of the series suggests the same general pattern over time.
Thus, while any point estimate of net undocumented immigration for a

Table 6.1

Annual Net Undocumented Immigration to California: Baseline Estimates Derived from IRS Tax Return Based Estimates of Domestic Migration

(in thousands)

April to April	Underlying Population Estimates					
	Series A	Series B	Series C	Series D	Series E	Series F
1980–81	82	12	159	118	119	130
1981–82	(52)	6	(16)	(21)	89	91
1982–83	16	(75)	(115)	(58)	71	80
1983–84	33	36	16	29	69	74
1984–85	17	104	95	72	74	83
1985–86	182	178	186	182	115	126
1986–87	288	190	226	235	123	133
1987–88	226	189	249	221	121	132
1988–89	239	259	266	254	232	239
1989–90	379	411	343	378	391	316
1990–91	291	332	147	257	279	159
1991–92	126	197	5	109	280	158
1992–93	2	113	95	70	242	190
1980–1985	97	183	139	140	422	458
1985–1990	1,313	1,226	1,270	1,270	983	946
1980–1990	1,410	1,409	1,409	1,409	1,404	1,404
1990–1993	418	642	247	436	801	507
1980–1993	1,828	2,051	1,656	1,845	2,206	1,911

SOURCE: Author's estimates.

NOTE: Baseline estimates vary according to underlying estimates (Series A through Series F) of annual population change. See Table 3.6 for underlying population estimates, and Appendix A for a discussion of the development of independent population estimates. See text for a discussion of the development of the baseline estimates.

Table 6.2

Annual Net Undocumented Immigration Estimates to California: Baseline Estimates Derived from Alternative Domestic Migration Estimates
(in thousands)

April to April		Underlying Population Estimates				
	Series A	Series B	Series C	Series D	Series E	Series F
1980–81	82	112	159	118	119	130
1981–82	(52)	6	(16)	(21)	89	91
1982–83	16	(75)	(115)	(58)	71	80
1983–84	33	36	16	29	69	74
1984–85	17	104	95	72	74	83
1985–86	182	178	186	182	115	126
1986–87	288	190	226	235	123	133
1987–88	226	189	249	221	121	132
1988–89	221	242	248	237	215	221
1989–90	317	349	281	315	329	254
1990–91	227	269	83	193	215	95
1991–92	88	160	(33)	71	242	120
1992–93	(27)	84	67	41	213	161
1980–1985	97	183	139	140	422	458
1985–1990	1,234	1,147	1,190	1,190	903	866
1980–1990	1,330	1,329	1,329	1,330	1,325	1,324
1990–1993	288	512	116	305	671	377
1980–1993	1,618	1,841	1,446	1,635	1,996	1,700

SOURCE: Author's estimates.
NOTE: Alternative domestic migration estimates incorporate some driver license address changes data. See discussion in text.

particular year is not reliable, the range of estimates for a particular year is reliable and the pattern over time is robust.

The tremendous increase in undocumented migration in the late 1980s is a methodological eventuality in this components-of-change approach with rapid population growth estimates in the late 1980s coupled with declining net domestic migration. The credibility of these results depends on the accuracy of each of the estimates of the components of population change. The following sections discuss the sensitivity of the undocumented migration estimates to alternative estimates of some components of change as well as alternative estimates of population change itself. As seen in Figure 6.2, point estimates of net undocumented immigration vary dramatically depending on which series of population estimates are used. In general, the overall level of the estimates over the 13-year period are most sensitive to assumptions regarding the undercount, while the annual levels are most sensitive to underlying population estimates.

Sensitivity to Undercount

Any increase in the net absolute undercount between 1980 and 1990 leads to an identical increase in the estimate of total net migration for the decade (as discussed in Chapter 5). The impact of the undercount upon net undocumented immigration estimates depends primarily on the level and secondarily on the timing of the undercount adjustment. Undercount adjustments will affect population estimates and domestic migration estimates, but will not change the natural increase nor the net legal immigration estimates. The effect on domestic migration estimates is relatively small, and operates through the adjustment of the unadjusted domestic migration tabulations to reflect total population. Thus, in this

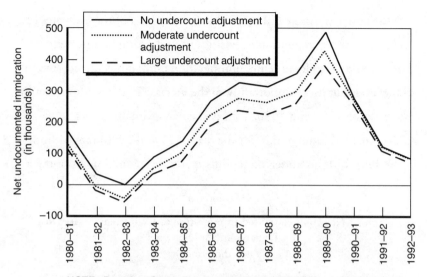

NOTE: Based on Series D population estimates. Moderate undercount adjustment assumes an increase in the net undercount rate from 3.0 percent in 1980 to 3.7 percent in 1990; large undercount adjustment assumes rates of 2.25 percent in 1980 and 4.5 percent in 1990.

Figure 6.2—Net Undocumented Immigration Estimates for California Under Various Net Undercount Assumptions

residual approach, the effect of undercount adjustments is felt most strongly in the estimate of net undocumented immigration.

As noted in Chapter 2, the level of the net undercount is uncertain. Here we consider two scenarios: first, a moderate increase in the net undercount (from 3.0 percent in 1980 to 3.7 percent in 1990), and second, a large increase (from 2.25 to 4.5 percent). The re-estimation of intercensal population estimates depends partly on the method used to allocate this undercount to individual years. Several scenarios are possible, but differences between the most plausible scenarios—in which the undercount adjustment is taken as a function of the estimated population—are not large.

As shown in Figure 6.2 and Table 6.3, the level of the estimates of undocumented immigration is sensitive to undercount adjustments. The increase in undocumented immigration estimates is directly related to the level, but more importantly to the increase in the net undercount rate between 1980 and 1990.[1] In particular, estimates of net undocumented immigration for the decade (1980–1990) ranged from 1.3 million with no undercount adjustment, to 1.7 million assuming a

Table 6.3

Annual Net Undocumented Immigration to California: Series with Undercount Adjustments (in thousands)

April to April	Underlying Population Estimates Adjusted for a Moderate Increase in the Undercount					
	Series A	Series B	Series C	Series D	Series E	Series F
1980–81	96	128	177	134	135	147
1981–82	(40)	20	(4)	(8)	107	109
1982–83	37	(61)	(104)	(43)	91	99
1983–84	54	57	37	49	86	92
1984–85	41	132	123	99	95	104
1985–86	219	213	222	218	142	152
1986–87	331	226	265	274	152	162
1987–88	265	227	290	261	153	163
1988–89	277	300	306	294	271	276
1989–90	425	460	386	424	438	357
1990–91	308	350	159	272	295	170
1991–92	138	211	18	122	297	174
1992–93	13	123	116	84	255	208
1980–1985	188	276	230	231	514	551
1985–1990	1,518	1,425	1,469	1,471	1,156	1,110
1980–1990	1,706	1,701	1,699	1,702	1,670	1,661
1990–1993	458	684	293	478	847	553
1980–1993	2,164	2,385	1,992	2,180	2,517	2,214

---

[1] For the post-1990 estimates, undercount adjustment factors were held constant at 1990 levels.

Table 6.3—continued

April to April	Underlying Population Estimates Adjusted for a Large Increase in the Undercount					
	Series A	Series B	Series C	Series D	Series E	Series F
1980–81	131	161	209	167	169	180
1981–82	(0)	58	35	31	142	144
1982–83	75	(20)	(61)	(2)	128	136
1983–84	90	93	73	85	121	126
1984–85	83	172	163	139	136	145
1985–86	264	258	267	263	189	200
1986–87	377	275	313	322	203	212
1987–88	316	278	340	311	207	217
1988–89	337	360	365	354	331	336
1989–90	485	519	447	484	498	419
1990–91	309	352	159	273	297	171
1991–92	138	211	16	122	298	174
1992–93	10	122	114	82	255	208
1980–1985	379	464	419	421	695	731
1985–1990	1,780	1,690	1,733	1,734	1,428	1,384
1980–1990	2,159	2,154	2,152	2,155	2,123	2,115
1990–1993	457	685	290	477	849	552
1980–1993	2,616	2,839	2,442	2,632	2,973	2,667

SOURCE: Author's estimates.

NOTE: Moderate undercount adjustment assumes an increase in the net undercount rate from 3.0 percent in 1980 to 3.7 percent in 1990; large undercount increase adjustment assumes rates of 2.25 percent in 1980 and 4.5 percent in 1990. See Table 3.6 for definition of underlying population estimates.

moderate (3.0 to 3.7 percent) undercount increase, to 2.2 million assuming a large undercount increase (2.25 percent to 4.5). Because the adjustment was taken as a linear function of estimated population, the patterns of change over time in estimated net undocumented migration are not affected. Thus, although the undercount adjustments here do not affect the annual pattern of change in undocumented immigration, the overall level of undocumented immigration is sensitive to undercount adjustments.

Sensitivity to Population Estimates

If we treat the population estimates developed by the California Department of Finance and the Census Bureau as exogenous, then the development of annual estimates of net undocumented migration is straightforward. Because the two series of population estimates are quite similar in the 1980s, the estimates of undocumented migration based on these population estimates are not dramatically different during that time frame. As the DOF and Census Bureau estimates of the state's population diverge in the early 1990s, the estimates of net undocumented migration produced here also diverge. However, because the DOF and Census Bureau estimates involve a components-of-change approach in which undocumented migration is assumed to be at a set level, the DOF and Census Bureau estimates are not independent estimates.[2] Numerous independent estimates of the total population of the state can be developed from administrative records which serve as indicators of the population (see Chapter 2 and Appendix A). The accuracy of each estimate depends on the strength of the correlation between the estimator and the actual population size. In particular, the estimates of undocumented migration depend on the estimator's ability to capture changes in the undocumented immigrant population of the state.

Figure 6.3 provides estimates of net undocumented migration based on six different estimates of the state's total population. The annual estimates of net undocumented migration are extremely sensitive to these

---

[2]The undocumented immigration estimates derived from the DOF and Census Bureau estimates of population change are included in this report despite the lack of independence. This inclusion is partly for illustrative purposes, but also stems from a desire to include a wide range of population estimates.

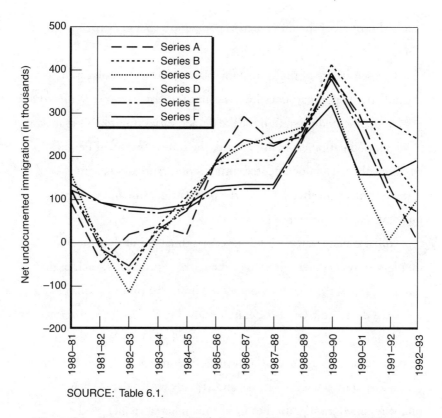

Net undocumented immigration (in thousands)

- - - - Series A
·········· Series B
············ Series C
-·-·-· Series D
-··-··- Series E
——— Series F

Figure 6.3—Estimates of Net Undocumented Immigration to California
Based on Alternative Population Estimates

different population estimates. The annual range of estimated net
undocumented migration varies from less than 100,000 in 1984–1985 to
almost 300,000 in 1991–1992. Indeed, almost all of the volatility in the
underlying population estimates is realized in the net undocumented
migration estimates. Annual estimates of natural increase and net legal
migration are invariant to the annual population estimates. Estimates of
domestic migration are partly a function of total population size, but
relative differences in total population are quite small. The components-
of-change methodology, with undocumented migration as the residual,

forces almost all of the difference in population change between the estimates into this residual number.

This sensitivity of the annual undocumented migration estimates to the underlying population estimates is not very satisfactory. While total net undocumented migration for the decade varies minimally regardless of which population estimator is used, the timing is quite different. In addition, the net undocumented immigration estimates become extremely unstable after 1990, as the population estimates diverge with no common final reference point.

Still, a general pattern if not level of annual net undocumented immigration is apparent in each of the series. Specifically, each of the estimates shows that net undocumented immigration to California increased during the late 1980s and declined in the early 1990s. If population growth accelerated in California during the late 1980s (and all the estimators suggest that it did) and if domestic migration declined (as suggested by the CPS, census, and IRS tax return data), then net undocumented immigration to California must have increased.

Finally, the population estimators used here are somewhat crude. Further refinement of the methods used to develop independent population estimates could narrow the range of these estimates. On the other hand, these crude estimators might more accurately indicate the true uncertainty regarding total population estimates.

Sensitivity to Other Components-of-Change Estimates

The sensitivity of the undocumented immigration estimates to alternative estimates of other components of change for any given year pale when compared with the sensitivity of the undocumented migration estimates to alternative underlying population estimates. Over time, however, the effect of alternative estimates of certain components can substantially alter long-term average levels.

Alternative Emigration Estimates

For example, emigration estimates 50-percent higher than those used in the baseline series will lead to an average annual increase in the undocumented migration estimates of only 18,000 per year during the 1980s and about 24,000 per year during the 1990s. Because emigration rates are taken as a proportion of legal immigration (and legal immigration does not change dramatically from year to year), the temporal pattern of net undocumented immigration estimates is not noticeably changed by alternative assumptions regarding emigration rates. The annual emigration numbers are not small, but they are much smaller than the uncertainty in the annual net undocumented immigration estimates associated with alternative population estimates. Nevertheless, any error in the level and timing of emigration estimates directly affects the estimates of undocumented immigration. And in the case of emigration, the long-term average estimates of net undocumented immigration are sensitive to various emigration assumptions. Increasing emigration rates by 50 percent, for example, leads to a 184,000 increase in undocumented immigration estimates for the decade (1980–1990) and an increase of 73,000 for the early 1990s. Under this scenario, the implied emigration rates for the 1980s would be a not implausible though somewhat high 33.75 percent (see the earlier discussion in Chapter 5 regarding emigration rates).

Alternative Special Agricultural Worker Estimates

Alternative treatment of SAWs could have a moderate impact on the estimates of undocumented immigration for 1987 and 1988. For example, assume that *all* of the amnestied SAWs in California reporting a last date of entry to the United States after June 1987 were establishing permanent or semi-permanent residence in California for the first time.[3] The estimates of net undocumented immigration would then be reduced by 37,000 in 1987–1988; 37,000 in 1988–1989; and less than 1,000 in 1989–1990.[4] The pattern of net undocumented immigration would not be seriously changed by such an assumption, and the sum of annual net undocumented immigration would be reduced by 76,000 for the decade. The effect of assumptions regarding SAWs could be even more dramatic if we assume widespread fraud in the program and believe that a large proportion of amnestied SAWs were actually first-time settlers in the United States.[5]

Alternative Domestic Migration Estimates

Any error in the estimates of net domestic migration translate into an equivalent error in the net undocumented migration estimates. In particular, the IRS tax return based estimates of domestic migration (those determined to be most reliable) are sensitive to differential weighting factors of domestic in-migrants versus domestic out-migrants. The census and CPS suggest that low-income persons and/or households

---

[3] The baseline estimates assume *half* of these SAWs were new residents.

[4] The assumption in the baseline estimates was that half of the SAWs reporting dates of entry after June 1987 were first-time settlers in the state.

[5] In this scenario, however, the estimates for 1987 and 1988 could be redefined as estimates of net undocumented immigration and SAWs given amnesty with fraudulent documents. In that case, the estimated numbers would remain unchanged.

are more heavily represented in the out-flows from the state in comparison with the in-flows. Adjustments for these domestic migration flows by income would lead to a decrease in estimates of net domestic migration, and thus to an increase in estimates of net undocumented immigration. Still, such an adjustment is minimal in light of the sensitivity of the undocumented immigration estimates to other assumptions.

An alternative series of domestic migration estimates (included in the baseline estimates) can be developed by using post 1987–1988 DLAC based estimates of domestic in-migration with IRS tax return based estimates of domestic out-migration. As discussed earlier, DLAC based estimates of domestic in-migration improved dramatically with the automation of DMV field offices in 1987–1988. Figure 6.4 shows the effect of these alternative domestic migration estimates on estimates of net undocumented immigration. The higher DLAC based estimates of domestic in-migration lead to lower estimates of net undocumented immigration. Table 6.2 provides net undocumented immigration estimates for each of the underlying population estimators using the alternative domestic migration estimates. The alternative domestic migration estimates imply lower levels of net undocumented immigration in the late 1980s and early 1990s, with a total decrease in net undocumented immigration of over 200,000. Two of the peak years of estimated net undocumented immigration, 1989–1990 and 1990–1991, each experience declines of over 60,000. Still, the pattern of net undocumented immigration remains essentially the same as in the baseline series.

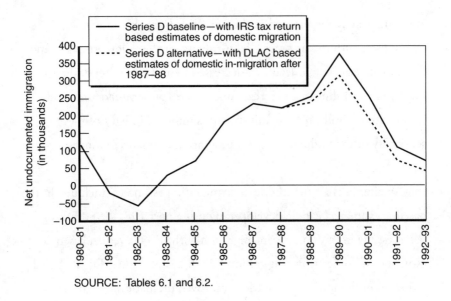

SOURCE: Tables 6.1 and 6.2.

Figure 6.4—Net Undocumented Immigration Estimates for California with Alternative Domestic Migration Estimates

Other Potential Errors

Finally, the effect of persons with non-immigrant visas remains to be discussed. In this methodological framework, persons who overstay non-immigrant visas will be considered undocumented immigrants. However, changes in the total number of residents with non-immigrant visas over time will bias these estimates. Any increase in long-term legal but not permanent (or semi-permanent) immigration will be incorrectly recorded as undocumented immigration.

7. Comparison with Other Estimates

In general, the estimates developed in this report are consistent with other estimates of long-run average annual changes in the undocumented immigrant population of California, but the short-run changes in the net flow developed here are contrary to the findings of some other researchers.

This study's estimates are unique in that the components of population change methodology employed allows for the estimation of *annual* net undocumented immigration. Most other estimates of net undocumented immigration are based on one of two methods: (1) the differencing of stock estimates from two points in time or (2) tabulations from retrospective questions on period of immigration to the United States. Such estimates are not strictly comparable to those developed here. Indeed, a differencing of stock estimates actually provides average annual change to the undocumented immigrant population rather than average annual net migration.[1] Similarly, estimates based on retrospective questions will exclude any previous immigrants who have since died.[2]

In this chapter we compare estimates developed in this report with the most current research in this area by the Urban Institute (Clark, Passel, Zimmerman, and Fix, 1994), Warren (1994), and Woodrow (1992). We also discuss studies by other researchers who have attempted to use apprehension data and field studies to evaluate the impact of IRCA and border enforcement on the flow of undocumented immigrants. Finally, the CPS can be used to estimate foreign immigration directly. We discuss those estimates in this chapter.

Comparisons with Urban Institute and Woodrow Estimates

The Urban Institute has developed estimates of undocumented immigrants in California counted in the 1990 census (Clark, Passel, Zimmerman, and Fix, 1994). Those estimates include the period of immigration for persons who were undocumented at the time of the 1990 census as well as for persons who arrived in an undocumented status but were later granted amnesty under the Immigration Reform and Control Act of 1986 (IRCA). The Urban Institute estimates of amnestied persons and undocumented immigrants can be combined to estimate undocumented migration by period of immigration (see Table

---

[1] Average annual change in the undocumented immigrant population equals average annual net migration of undocumented immigrants less average annual deaths to undocumented immigrants.

[2] Such estimates also do not include any immigrants who have since emigrated. However, because the estimates of undocumented immigration developed here are net estimates, the exclusion of emigrants is consistent with the approach used here.

7.1). This measure of undocumented immigration is not strictly comparable to the estimates developed in this report, since it represents persons counted in the 1990 census. Some undocumented immigrants who came to California during the 1980s died prior to the 1990 census, and therefore would not be included in the census or the Urban Institute estimate. Because the recently arrived undocumented immigrant population is quite young, such mortality is likely to be very low and not a significant source of difference between the Urban Institute estimates and those developed in this report. The Urban Institute based estimates of persons counted in the census who came to the United States as undocumented immigrants during the 1980s and who lived in California in 1990 is 1,330,000. Estimates developed in this report of undocumented immigration for 1980–1990 based solely on census counts range from 1,324,000 to 1,410,000. Given the different methodologies used for the Urban Institute estimates and the estimates developed in this report, the close agreement between the two estimates is reassuring.

Other estimates developed in this report that include undercount adjustments range from 1,578,000 to 2,159,000, indicating a census undercount rate of between 12 percent and 38 percent for undocumented immigrant residents arriving during the 1980s.[3] Combining Warren's estimate of the total number of undocumented immigrants in California in 1990 with the Urban Institute's estimates of undocumented immigrants counted in the 1990 census produces a net undercount rate of 22 percent. Woodrow-Lafield (1995) cites a "preferred" undercount rate of undocumented immigrant residents of 30

---

[3]Alternative underlying assumptions, discussed in Chapter 6, would lead to a wider range.

Table 7.1

Comparison of Undocumented Immigration Estimates for California

Period of Immigration	Urban Institute Estimates (in thousands)				PPIC Estimates (in thousands)
	Undocumented Immigrants Counted in the 1990 Census	SAW Residents Less SAW Emigrants	LAW Immigrants Less LAW Emigrants	Total: Undocumented Immigrants plus IRCA Amnestied Persons	Low to High Estimates
1980–81	109	13	289	411	30 to 221
1982–84	29	113	20	162	–4 to 237
1985–86	113	203	4	320	238 to 470
1987–90	351	86	—	437	607 to 859
1980–90 Total	602	415	313	1,330	1,324 to 1,410

SOURCE: Urban Institute estimates derived from Clark, Passel, Zimmerman, and Fix (1994), *Fiscal Impacts of Undocumented Aliens: Selected Estimates for Seven States*, Washington, D.C.: The Urban Institute, Appendix A, "Data and Methods for Estimating the Number of Undocumented Immigrants in the 1990 Census."

NOTE: PPIC estimates are those developed in this report based on 12 series shown in Tables 6.1 and 6.2.

percent in the 1990 census, but points out that, depending on the number of undocumented immigrant residents and the coverage of legal immigrant residents, undercount rates could be much higher or lower. The estimates developed here that include undercount adjustments are consistent with the implied and estimated undercount rates for all undocumented immigrants.

Despite the close agreement between the Urban Institute based decennial estimates of undocumented immigration and those developed in this report, the estimates for specific time frames in the 1980s are in disagreement. In particular, the Urban Institute estimates imply very high levels of undocumented immigration in 1980 and 1981 whereas the estimates developed here suggest that undocumented immigration was relatively low during those years. The higher Urban Institute numbers for 1980 and 1981 are driven by the large number of IRCA applicants who reported arriving in 1980 and 1981. To be eligible for the general amnesty program under IRCA, formerly undocumented immigrants must have lived in the United States since January 1, 1982. Most persons applied for amnesty in 1987 and 1988. To the extent that persons entered the United States after 1982 and filed for amnesty under the general provisions of IRCA, the Urban Institute numbers will be biased high for 1980 and 1981. If the estimates developed in this report are accurate, then misreporting of year of entry did occur among those applying for amnesty under the general provisions of IRCA.

One key finding of this report is that net undocumented immigration actually increased after the passage of IRCA. However, the Urban Institute based estimates for 1987–1990 are lower than those developed here, and suggest that undocumented immigration declined after the passage of IRCA.

The estimates developed by Woodrow (1992) are point-in-time estimates for the entire United States for June 1986, June 1988, and November 1989. Using a residual technique in which undocumented immigrants are estimated as the difference between various Current Population Survey estimates of the foreign born population and estimates of legal residents for the same points in time, Woodrow develops estimates of average annual change in the undocumented immigrant population for several time periods. Comparing her recent estimates with previous CPS and census based estimates, Woodrow finds a pattern of change in the undocumented immigrant population that suggests net increases were highest between 1986 and 1988, but quite low from 1988 to 1989. Since the estimates are based on a differencing of stock estimates, they are not strictly comparable to the estimates developed here. Also, because the estimates are for the entire United States, the patterns of change might suggest what we would expect in California, but the levels do not. Woodrow's nationwide estimates suggest very different patterns for undocumented immigrants from Latin America compared to those born in other regions, and very different patterns for undocumented immigrants entering after 1981 versus those entering the United States from 1960 to 1981.

Specifically, among those entering after 1981, Woodrow finds a large increase in the undocumented immigrant population between June 1988 (about 700,000) and November 1989 (1.4 million). Such a large increase is consistent with the estimates developed here. However, Woodrow's estimate of a large decline between June 1988 and November 1989 in the undocumented immigrant population that entered between 1960 and 1981 offsets most of this increase. Woodrow further finds that much of the increase could be attributed to an increase in the undocumented immigrant population from Latin America, and estimates annualized levels of annual change in the Latin American undocumented immigrant population of 531,000 in 1988 and 1989. This figure compares to an annualized decline of 486,000 in the number of undocumented immigrants born in other regions of the world over this same period. Because Latin Americans undoubtedly comprise a higher share of California's flow of undocumented immigration than in the rest of the country, this finding suggests that net undocumented immigration to California might have been higher than net undocumented immigration to the rest of the country in 1988 and 1989.[4] In general, some of Woodrow's estimates for the nation are consistent with the patterns for California developed in this report, but other estimates developed by Woodrow are not consistent with those developed here.

Studies of the Effect of IRCA on the Flow of Undocumented Immigration

Numerous researchers have attempted to measure the impact of IRCA on undocumented immigration to the United States (Bean, Espenshade, White, and Dymowski, 1990; Espenshade, 1990; Crane, Asch, Heilbrunn, and Cullinane, 1990; Donato, Durand, and Massey, 1992a; Massey, Donato, and Liang, 1990; Lowell and Jing, 1994; Gonzalez and Escobar, 1990). Some have based their analyses on apprehension data; others have used other indicators of undocumented immigration. The findings are mixed: Some suggest large reductions in

---

[4]Another caveat of Woodrow's estimates is that if the decline in the 1960–1981 cohort was due to mortality, then the total numbers are in fact consistent. However, mortality probably plays a small role in the large declines observed.

the flow of undocumented immigrants to the United States due to IRCA; others find no impact. Researchers who use apprehension data tend to find large reductions in the flow of undocumented immigration due to IRCA (Bean, Espenshade, White, and Dymowski, 1990; Espenshade, 1990; Crane, Asch, Heilbrunn, and Cullinane, 1990). Researchers who use other indicators, including field studies of primary sending communities in Mexico, find little or no impact of IRCA (Cornelius, 1989; Crane, Asch, Heilbrunn, and Cullinane, 1990; Donato, Durand, and Massey, 1992a; Massey, Donato, and Liang, 1990; Lowell and Jing, 1994; Gonzalez and Escobar, 1990). The estimates of net undocumented immigration developed in this report suggest an increase in net undocumented immigration after the passage of IRCA.

Apprehension data for the San Diego sector suggest a decline in the number of unauthorized border crossings for several years, but the number of apprehensions remained quite high. Indeed, the number of apprehensions in each of the two years after the passage of IRCA in 1986 are higher than for any year prior to 1986 (see Figure 7.1). However, by federal fiscal year 1988–1989, the number of apprehensions in the San Diego sector was 42 percent lower than it was in 1985–1986. While the number of apprehensions along the border is a function not only of the number of unauthorized crossings but also border enforcement,[5] a decline in apprehensions is generally taken as an indication that the gross flow of undocumented immigrants into the United States has also declined.

---

[5]That is, the number of agents along the border, border enforcement resources, and the efficiency of those agents and resources.

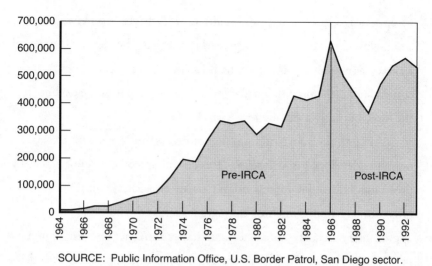

700,000
600,000
500,000
400,000
300,000
200,000
100,000
0

Pre-IRCA

Post-IRCA

1964 1966 1968 1970 1972 1974 1976 1978 1980 1982 1984 1986 1988 1990 1992

SOURCE: Public Information Office, U.S. Border Patrol, San Diego sector.

Figure 7.1—Apprehensions of Undocumented Immigrants, San Diego Sector

In general, research on the flow of undocumented immigrants based on apprehension data suggests that the flow of undocumented immigrants to the United States declined immediately after the passage of IRCA. Bean et al. (1990) estimate that between the passage of IRCA in November 1986 and September 1989 apprehensions at the border were 47 percent lower than they would have been in the absence of IRCA. The authors attribute about half of the reduction in apprehensions to the legalization of seasonal agricultural workers, which allowed these formerly undocumented immigrants to cross the border legally (Bean, Espenshade, White, and Dymowski, 1990). Espenshade (1990) uses a repeated trials model of undocumented immigration based on apprehension data and concludes that IRCA reduced the gross flow of undocumented immigrants to the United States 44 percent from November 1986 to September 1987, and 30 percent from November 1987 to September 1988 over what would have been expected in the absence of IRCA. Crane et al. (1990) examine border apprehensions along with counts of persons aggregating along the border, visa data, and a survey of employers to determine if IRCA had an effect. They conclude that the preponderance of evidence points to some decline in the flow, but only a small one.

Although the above findings do not necessarily agree with the estimates developed in this report, this lack of agreement is not especially problematic. Even if apprehension data are an accurate measure of the gross flows of undocumented immigrants across the border, apprehension data are not an accurate indicator of net undocumented immigration to the United States. The most serious problems with the use of apprehension data to measure undocumented immigration include:

- Many undocumented immigrants do not come to the United States via unauthorized border crossings; Warren (1994) estimates that over half of the undocumented immigrants in the United States in 1992 had entered the United States legally with a non-immigrant visa. Warren and Passel (1987) estimate that only 55 percent of undocumented immigrants counted in the 1980 census were from Mexico.

- Even if border apprehensions adequately measure flows into the United States, they are not able to capture flows out of the United States. To determine net migration, it is necessary to measure return flows from the United States to Mexico and other countries of origin of undocumented immigrants.

- The flow of undocumented immigrants into the United States across the border is dominated by short-term and cyclical migrants, not permanent settlers. A 1994 study of Operation Hold-the-Line in El Paso by University of Texas researchers

(Bean et al., 1994) found that despite a dramatic decline in apprehensions, long-distance labor migration was not significantly affected. It is possible that IRCA reduced the flow of short-term and cyclical migrants but did not deter more long-term migration.

• The number of illegal border crossings and thus apprehensions should have declined after IRCA as a result of the legalization program. About three million amnestied persons were removed from the potential pool of illegal crossers. Perhaps half of the decline in border apprehensions can be attributed to the legalization of this population (Bean et al., 1990).

Other research based on the impact of IRCA on the flow of undocumented immigrants has found little or no impact. Taylor (1993) used California Employment Development Department data for farmworkers from 1984 to 1990, and found no evidence that IRCA reduced the number of immigrants coming to work in California agriculture. Martin (1990a) states that since IRCA, labor intensive agriculture has actually *expanded* and employers have *not* needed to implement programs that would have allowed for the legal importation of more farmworkers. In its 1992 report, the U.S. Commission on Agricultural Workers concluded that IRCA did not successfully reduce undocumented immigration and that the "continuing influx of unauthorized workers" has in large part "frustrated the development of a stable farm labor market with improved wages and working conditions" (p. 15). Based on data from the National Agricultural Workers Survey, the Department of Labor concluded that from 1989 through 1991 the U.S. farm labor force became increasingly dependent on Latin American and undocumented immigrants. Data from the survey also indicate a decline in real hourly wages of 14 percent for farmworkers hired through labor contractors and 3 percent for other farmworkers (U.S. Department of Labor, 1993).[6] Lowell and Jing (1994) noted a *lack* of marked change of employers' hiring practices after the passage of IRCA, and cited the prevalence of false documents as one reason employers may still be hiring undocumented immigrants.[7]

Field research in Mexican sending communities also indicates that IRCA has not successfully reduced the flow of undocumented immigrants. Using data from the Mexican Migration Project, Donato, Durand, and Massey find no evidence that IRCA deterred undocumented immigration from seven Mexican sending communities (Donato et al., 1992a). Further work by Donato, Durand, and Massey on the impact of IRCA on labor conditions led to the conclusion that rather than deterring undocumented immigration, "IRCA appears simply to have spurred the growth of an underground economy" (Donato et al., 1992b, p. 111). Indeed, some field research suggests that flows have increased since the passage of IRCA (Cornelius, 1989; Massey, Donato, and Liang, 1990; Gonzalez and Escobar, 1990). In their study of migration from a municipality in Mexico, Gonzalez and Escobar state:

> It was very evident, both in Jalostotitlán and other migrant towns, that for just $350, individuals could purchase "employer's letters" stating that they had been working in agriculture, although it was obvious that many Jaleños had never devoted themselves to this activity during their working lives. For this reason, from 1987 to 1989, there was a significant rise in the number of illegal migrants who left their homes for the sole purpose of regularizing their immigration status in the United States (p. 14).

---

[6]Undocumented immigrants are more likely to be hired through farm labor contractors than are workers with other legal statuses.

[7]The Immigration and Naturalization Service estimates that prior to the enactment of IRCA it seized fewer than 25,000 counterfeit documents annually. Since the enactment of IRCA, the INS seizes several hundred thousand counterfeit documents each year. In one raid alone in 1993 in Los Angeles, the INS seized over 100,000 counterfeit documents (Johnson, 1994).

Cornelius (1989) concludes from a 1988–1989 survey conducted in three rural Mexican communities that immigration, both legal and undocumented, to the United States was higher in 1988 than in any previous year, and that "IRCA may have kept more Mexicans in the United States than it has either kept out or forced to return home" (Cornelius, 1989, p. 699). Massey, Donato, and Liang (1990) analyze migration data up to 1988 from two sending communities in Mexico, and find that the highest probability of out-migration in any year since 1975 occurred after the passage of IRCA.

CPS Direct Estimates

Estimates of total foreign immigration to California can be developed directly from the CPS through the migration question based on location of residence one year prior to the survey. The location of residence one year prior to the survey was asked in the March surveys of 1981 through 1984 and 1986 through 1995.

CPS estimates of foreign immigration over the past year less estimates of legal immigration provide estimates of undocumented immigration. As with the estimates of domestic migration from the CPS, these estimates are highly imprecise due to small sample sizes and must be interpreted with caution due to weighting issues. As shown in Table 7.2, the general pattern of undocumented immigration suggested by these estimates is similar to the pattern developed in this report, with relatively low levels of undocumented immigration in the early 1980s, high levels in the late 1980s, and sharply declining levels in the early

Table 7.2

Comparing Current Population Survey Estimates to Legal Foreign Immigration for California

CPS Year	International Migrants to CA, CPS Estimates	Period	Legal Immigration, DOF Tabulations of INS Data Adjusted to April	Implied Undocumented
1982	230,556	1981–82	170,500	60,056
1983	210,098	1982–83	149,000	61,098
1984	231,843	1983–84	137,500	94,343
1986	334,715	1985–86	161,500	173,215
1987	306,651	1986–87	164,000	142,651
1988	286,187	1987–88	173,500	112,687
1989	493,857	1988–89	183,500	310,357
1990	412,471	1989–90	182,500	229,971
1991	411,191	1990–91	189,000	222,191
1992	324,073	1991–92	215,000	109,073
1993	258,728	1992–93	242,000	16,728

SOURCE: Author's calculations.

1990s. The point estimates are extremely imprecise, however, with 90-percent confidence intervals of about ±90,000 for most years.[8]

In sum, other studies that attempt to place undocumented immigration at discrete points in time find results similar to those developed here for long-term average annual estimates. However, estimates for specific shorter term time frames are not always in agreement. In particular, estimates developed by the Urban Institute, while not wholly comparable, do not show the same large increase in the late 1980s that are estimated here. The Urban Institute estimates rely on retrospective data on period of immigration; misreporting of period of entry among IRCA applicants could induce errors in those estimates.

---

[8]The period 1988–1989 is an exception, with a 90-percent confidence interval of about ±140,000.

Woodrow's estimates suggest that certain populations of undocumented immigrants (those from Latin America and those in the cohort arriving after 1981) may have experienced large net population increases in the late 1980s, but those increases were largely offset by declines in other undocumented immigrant populations. Studies of the impact of IRCA reach various conclusions: Some studies suggest that IRCA has had no impact and others suggest that IRCA led to a decline in the flow of undocumented immigrants to the United States in the late 1980s. Those studies that found IRCA had an impact rely on border apprehensions, which do not include the large proportion of undocumented immigrants who are visa overstayers and do not allow for the estimation of *net* undocumented immigration. Some field studies suggest that flows might have actually increased since IRCA. The CPS estimates are imprecise but consistent with those developed here.

8. Some Possible Explanations

According to the temporal patterns of net undocumented immigration developed in this study, undocumented immigration increased as California's economy improved in the mid 1980s and increased further after the passage of IRCA in the late 1980s. With the recession in the early 1990s, net undocumented immigration to California declined. This chapter provides a descriptive and speculative discussion of the observed patterns of undocumented immigration in light of IRCA and economic factors. The chapter first discusses economic factors, then turns to the potential effect of IRCA.

Economic Factors

California experienced strong job growth in the mid to late 1980s, and slow-to-negative job growth in the early 1980s and early 1990s (see Figure 8.1). In general, low levels of net undocumented immigration coincide with periods of slow employment growth in California, and high levels of undocumented immigration coincide with periods of high

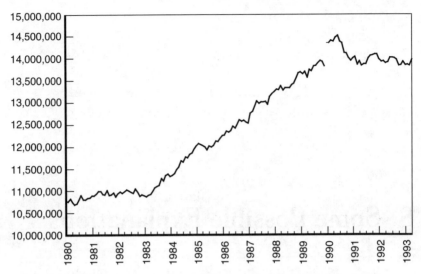

SOURCE: California Employment Development Department, *Civilian Labor Force, Employment, and Unemployment; 1980–Current (March 1994 Benchmark)*, January 22, 1996.

NOTE: Data for years prior to 1990 are not comparable to data for 1990 and subsequent years due to the introduction of 1990 census population data.

Figure 8.1—California Employment: Seasonally Adjusted

employment growth. Economic conditions in Mexico, the primary country of origin of undocumented immigrants to California,[1] also appear to be consistent with the patterns of undocumented immigration developed in this study.

In particular, in the early 1980s employment growth was slow. In the first three years of the decade, total employment in California increased only 1.1 percent (California Employment Development Department, 1996). Exchange rates between Mexican pesos and U.S. dollars did not change much until 1982, and real wages for

---

[1]Warren (1994) estimates that 67 percent of California's undocumented immigrant population in 1992 was from Mexico.

manufacturing labor in Mexico were relatively constant (see Figure 8.2). Net undocumented immigration was at relatively low levels during this period.

In the mid 1980s, increasing levels of net undocumented immigration coincided with both strong employment growth in California and declining relative real wages in manufacturing production in Mexico (see Figures 8.1 and 8.2). The value of the peso relative to the dollar declined dramatically during this period. In the late 1980s, employment growth in California remained strong. Net undocumented immigration levels peaked in the late 1980s, although real wages for manufacturing labor in Mexico increased during this same time period.

In the early 1990s, net undocumented immigration declined substantially. Several of the series of estimates suggest that by 1992–

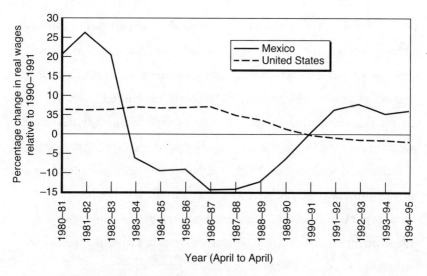

SOURCE: Hanson and Spilimbergo (1996).

Figure 8.2—Trends in U.S. and Mexican Real Wages

1993 net undocumented immigration to California was less than 125,000 persons. The estimated decline in net undocumented immigration in the early 1990s coincides with both a period of slow or negative employment growth in California and a period of increasing wages in Mexico (see Figures 8.1 and 8.2).

IRCA

Each of the series of estimates of net undocumented immigration developed in this report suggests that the greatest net flow occurred from 1988 through 1990. Although economic factors might have played an important role in the increase in undocumented immigration in the mid 1980s and the decline in the early 1990s, economic factors alone do not appear to explain the peak in undocumented immigration observed in the late 1980s.

Our preliminary analysis suggests that there were no remarkable changes in wage and employment opportunities that could explain the estimated increase in net undocumented immigration in the late 1980s. Indeed, as shown in Figure 8.2, real wages in the United States for production occupations in seven industries were declining relative to real wages in manufacturing production labor in Mexico at the same time (Hanson and Spilimbergo, 1996). Although average annual employment in California was increasing at a rapid rate in the late 1980s (over 3 percent per year based on California Employment Development Department estimates), employment increases in California were also strong in the mid 1980s. The increase in net undocumented immigration in the late 1980s occurred shortly after the passage of IRCA, as formerly undocumented immigrant residents applied for and received legal residency status. This increase in immigration could be related to IRCA in one or more ways:

- Adjustment to legal status may have encouraged many IRCA applicants' families and/or friends, living abroad at the time of the passage of IRCA, to move to the United States in an undocumented status. In California, 1.6 million persons applied for amnesty.

- Increased difficulty in crossing the border illegally, or a perceived increase in the difficulty of doing so, may have led those who had illegally crossed the border to spend more time in the United States.[2]

- IRCA might have allowed easier undocumented immigration to the United States. Under the Special Agricultural Workers provisions of IRCA, individuals could claim at the U.S. border that they qualified for legalization (even without proof of work in U.S. agriculture) and obtain 90-day entry and work permits (Martin, 1990a).

The first scenario is the most likely one to result in the large increases in net undocumented immigration estimated in this report. The importance of social networks in international migration is well known. Whether legal residents serve as a greater magnet than undocumented residents for friends and relatives is not known, but it seems reasonable. In a survey of three rural Mexican sending communities in 1988–1989, Cornelius (1989) found that men granted amnesty began sending for their wives and children in Mexico. Cornelius also cites other evidence

---

[2]Based on Mexico's 1978 *National Survey of Emigration to the Northern Border and to the United States*, Kossoudji (1992) found that an increase in the probability of apprehensions led to an increase in time in the United States per trip and a decrease in time in Mexico and in trips to Mexico.

that IRCA led to an increase in immigration because of family reunification, including large increases in the number of women and children crossing the border, and a 48 percent increase in applicants for temporary visas at the U.S. Consulate in Tijuana during the post-IRCA period, fueled primarily by dependents of persons who were granted amnesty under IRCA. For the entire United States, Woodrow-Lafield (1994) notes that relatives of IRCA-amnestied persons filed over 800,000 petitions for immigrant visas as of January 1994. The INS has testified in Congress that most of the spouses and minor children applying for visas to join amnestied residents are already in the United States (*Migration News*, June 1996).

A survey of persons given amnesty under the general provisions of IRCA suggests that social networks could be a powerful magnet for large numbers of undocumented immigrants. In the households of the 753,000 general amnesty applicants in 1992, there were 665,000 persons who had lived elsewhere several years earlier (at the time of amnesty application between May 5, 1987 and May 4, 1988).[3] Of those new household members, over 250,000 were reported to have an unknown or other-than-legal immigration status. Over 10 percent of Californians were general amnesty applicants or residents of households with general amnesty applicants. If we consider SAWs, for which no survey data are available, the numbers would be even higher.

---

[3] Weighted estimates based on the author's calculations from the Legalized Population Survey Public Use File. For over half the sample (2,182 of 4,012), California was the state of residence. Persons who lived elsewhere could have lived abroad or in another household in the United States.

Discussion

In general, the estimated increase in net undocumented immigration in the late 1980s may be related to expanded social networks in conjunction with employment opportunities. Changes in estimated net undocumented immigration for other periods are consistent with economic trends in California and Mexico. If the increase in undocumented immigration in the late 1980s was driven by persons joining amnestied family members, then it was a unique event driven by a particular public policy (IRCA) and is not likely to be replicated in the future. It is worth noting that many, if not most, of the undocumented immigrants who were joining family members will eventually become legal permanent residents through family reunification provisions of U.S. immigration law.

The above discussion is speculative. In particular, whereas Mexico is the leading country of origin of undocumented immigrants to California, a substantial share of undocumented immigrants come from other countries. Only a few broadly defined measures have been included in this discussion. Changes in the levels of net undocumented immigration could be related to economic and political factors not considered here.

9. Conclusion

The annual estimates of net undocumented immigration produced in this residual-components-of-change approach highlight the inherent problems in indirect measures of a population. The accuracy of these estimates is dependent on numerous assumptions and the accuracy of the components of population change as well as the accuracy of estimates of population change itself.

The annual estimates indicate that net undocumented immigration to California increased from the early 1980s to the late 1980s, and declined in the early 1990s. The level of the estimates is subject to much uncertainty. If population growth did accelerate in California during the late 1980s, and all the estimators suggest that it did, and if domestic migration declined (as suggested by the most reliable data we have on domestic migration), then net undocumented immigration to California must have increased in the late 1980s. While the point estimates of net undocumented immigration for any given year are not reliable, the pattern of change over time does appear to be robust.

The broad ranges of the annual estimates of net undocumented immigration are primarily due to uncertainty regarding annual population change. The various population estimators used here are somewhat crude. Nevertheless, the differences between the total population estimates are small; it is only the differences in the estimates of annual change that are sizable. While further refinement of the methods used to develop independent population estimates could narrow the range of these estimates, it is plausible that these differences adequately reflect the uncertainty of annual population estimates.

The patterns of net undocumented immigration developed in this report are consistent with economic and policy explanations. Specifically, periods of relatively high levels of undocumented immigration coincide with periods of strong employment growth in California, whereas periods with relatively low or decreasing levels of undocumented immigration coincide with slow or negative employment growth in the state. The highest estimated levels of net undocumented immigration occurred in the late 1980s and might be related to IRCA. Further research is necessary to evaluate the effect of IRCA and economic factors.

Most important, these estimates represent the first set of estimates of annual net undocumented immigration to California. The estimates show that the net flow of undocumented immigrants fluctuates widely over time. In addition to coinciding with economic conditions and possibly the implementation of IRCA, variation in the number of undocumented immigrants coincides with and contributes to periods of both rapid and slow population growth in the state.

Appendix A

Development of Independent Population Estimates

Six series of independent population estimates were developed in this study, and three (Series A, Series B, and Series C) are included in the components-of-change analysis in the main body of the report. An additional series, Series D, represents an average of Series A, Series B, and Series C, and is also included in the main body of the report. The estimates are derived from various indirect measures of the state's population, and rely on administrative data in conjunction with census counts to estimate annual populations. All of the estimates are based on censal ratio estimation methods in which ratios of administrative records data to census populations are established for 1980 and 1990. Intercensal populations are developed by applying linearly interpolated ratios to intercensal administrative data. For the estimates beyond 1990, some ratios were held constant at 1990 levels while others continued the trend. Where appropriate, the counts and thus the ratios are age or race/ethnic specific.

As can be seen in Table A.1, the series can be divided into two groups: those that are derived from age-specific indicators, and those that are derived from total population indicators. Series A, B, G, and H are developed from age-specific indicators of the population. These series use the same indicators of populations aged 17 and under and aged 65 and over. Populations aged 18 to 64 are determined by licensed drivers in Series A, occupied households in Series B, employment in Series G, and labor force in Series H. Population estimates in Series C and Series I are derived for all age groups.

The accuracy of the estimates depends on the strength and stability of the relationship between the administrative data and the population

Table A.1

Indicators of Population Used in Intercensal and Post-Censal Population Estimates

Series	Age Group			
	0–4	5–17	18–64	65+
A	Births	School enrollment	Licensed drivers	Medicare enrollment
B	Births	School enrollment	Occupied households	Medicare enrollment
C	All ages: persons per occupied housing unit and group quarters populations			
D	Average of Series A, Series B, and Series C			
G	Births	School enrollment	Employment	Medicare enrollment
H	Births	School enrollment	Labor force	Medicare enrollment
I	All ages: vital rates method using births and deaths			

NOTE: Series E and Series F are based on state estimates developed by the U.S. Census Bureau and the California Department of Finance.

group estimated by those data. In general, constant ratios over time between the population and the indicator will produce more reliable estimates. Table A.2 provides censal ratios for some of the indicators used to develop independent population estimates. Of course, with only two data points, it is not possible to identify stability, although it is possible to identify ratios that have changed substantially between 1980 and 1990. Ratios at or near 1.0 suggest that the administrative data coverage of the population is high. According to these criteria, kindergarten through grade 12 enrollment is a better indicator of the population aged 5 through 17 than is grade 1 through grade 10 enrollment (the ratio for kindergarten through grade 12 enrollment is closer to or even higher than 1.0 and changes less between 1980 and

Table A.2

Censal Ratios for Administrative Data

	1980	1990
Population aged 0–4: births during the past five years	0.97	0.95
Population aged 5–17: kindergarten–grade 12 enrollment	1.05	0.99
Population aged 5–17: Grade 1–Grade 10 enrollment	1.50	1.37
Population aged 18–64: licensed drivers ages 18-64	1.04	1.04
Population aged 18–64: occupied housing units	1.72	1.81
Population aged 18–64: employment (CPS based series)	1.28	1.24
Population aged 18-64: employment (payroll series)	n/a	1.24
Population aged 18-64: labor force	1.38	1.32
Population aged 65 and over: Medicare enrollment	1.03	1.04
Population aged 65 and over: deaths	13.0	14.6
Household population: occupied housing units	2.68	2.75
Total population: births	49.17	59.05
Total population: deaths	140.41	127.57

SOURCES: Birth and death data: California Department of Health Services and the California Department of Finance (unpublished tables); School enrollments: California Department of Finance (unpublished tables); Housing units and household population: California Department of Finance (Report E-8090); Labor force and employment: California Employment Development Department bulletin board; Medicare enrollment: California Department of Finance (unpublished table).

1990). Licensed drivers appear to be both the most complete and constant indicators of the population aged 18 to 64, and Medicare enrollment appears to be the best measure of the population aged 65 and over.

Table A.3 provides annual population estimates for each of the series. Table A.4 and Figure A.1 show estimates of annual population change generated by each of the series. Series A, Series B, and Series C were included in the final set of estimates used to generate undocumented immigration estimates. Series A uses a relatively complete measure of the population aged 18 to 64, licensed drivers. Series B and Series C use estimates of occupied households. Persons per occupied household did not change substantially between 1980 and 1990, and occupied housing units are less susceptible to business-cycle effects than are employment and labor force data.

Series G and Series H were not included in the final set of estimates. These series are susceptible to business-cycle fluctuations and probably overstate population growth or decline. For example, because of strong job growth in 1989–1990, both the employment series (Series G) and the labor force series (Series H) suggest extremely rapid population growth in 1989–1990. The exclusion of these series is a conservative choice in light of the principal findings of this study. The patterns of undocumented immigration observed over time would be more dramatic with these underlying population estimates.

Series I, the vital rates method, was also excluded from the final set of independent population estimates used in this report. As shown in Table A.2, the ratios of population to births and to deaths is very high and changed substantially between 1980 and 1990. The series estimates, as shown in Figure A.1, are volatile. While births might be a good

Table A.3

Annual Estimates of Population for California

April 1 Estimate	Series A	Series B	Series C	Series D	Series G	Series H	Series I
1980	23,668,000	23,668,000	23,668,000	23,668,000	23,668,000	23,668,000	23,668,000
1981	24,116,000	24,147,000	24,194,000	24,152,000	24,048,000	24,053,000	23,975,000
1982	24,495,000	24,583,000	24,608,000	24,562,000	24,623,000	24,634,000	24,265,000
1983	24,969,000	24,966,000	24,952,000	24,962,000	24,855,000	24,872,000	24,506,000
1984	25,425,000	25,425,000	25,391,000	25,414,000	25,390,000	25,413,000	25,103,000
1985	25,927,000	26,014,000	25,970,000	25,970,000	26,011,000	26,041,000	25,940,000
1986	26,627,000	26,710,000	26,674,000	26,670,000	26,637,000	26,674,000	26,328,000
1987	27,453,000	27,437,000	27,438,000	27,443,000	27,317,000	27,362,000	27,071,000
1988	28,230,000	28,177,000	28,239,000	28,215,000	27,970,000	28,025,000	28,086,000
1989	28,967,000	28,935,000	29,003,000	28,968,000	28,651,000	28,713,000	29,007,000
1990	29,760,000	29,760,000	29,760,000	29,760,000	29,760,000	29,760,000	29,760,000

NOTE: See Table A.1 and text for descriptions of the series.

113

Table A.4

Annual Estimates of Population Change for California

April to April Change	Series A	Series B	Series C	Series D	Series G	Series H	Series I
1980–81	448,000	479,000	526,000	484,000	380,000	386,000	307,000
1981–82	378,000	436,000	415,000	410,000	575,000	581,000	291,000
1982–83	474,000	383,000	343,000	400,000	233,000	238,000	240,000
1983–84	457,000	459,000	440,000	452,000	535,000	541,000	597,000
1984–85	502,000	589,000	579,000	556,000	620,000	628,000	837,000
1985–86	700,000	696,000	704,000	700,000	626,000	634,000	388,000
1986–87	825,000	727,000	764,000	772,000	680,000	688,000	744,000
1987–88	777,000	740,000	801,000	773,000	653,000	663,000	1,015,000
1988–89	737,000	757,000	764,000	753,000	680,000	688,000	921,000
1989–90	793,000	825,000	757,000	792,000	1,109,000	1,047,000	753,000

NOTE: See Table A.1 and text for descriptions of the series.

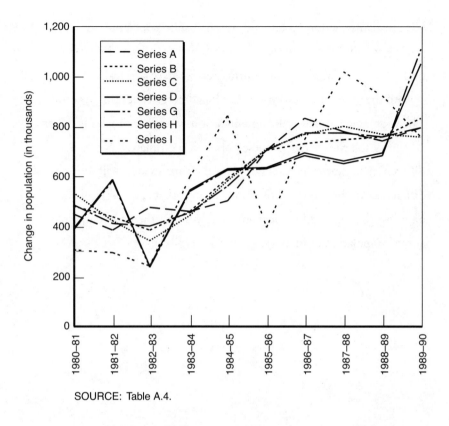

SOURCE: Table A.4.

Figure A.1—Annual Estimates of Population Change for California

indicator of persons in prime child-bearing ages, and deaths might be a good indicator of the elderly population, these indicators do not reflect changes in populations of other very large age groups. Inclusion of race/ethnic-specific vital events and populations did not improve the series.

An additional method and data source, not shown in Table A.1 or Table A.2, distributes total population change for the decade based on residential building permits authorized. The population estimates produced via this method are volatile. The permits data reflect business/construction cycles, and thus overstate population growth during periods of much economic and construction activity, and understate population growth during recessionary periods.

All the population estimates developed here are admittedly crude. The wide range of net undocumented immigration estimates is driven largely by the wide range of these population estimates. Nevertheless, the differences between the total population estimates are small; it is only the differences in the estimates of annual change that are sizable. It is plausible that these differences adequately reflect the uncertainty of annual population estimates.

References

Ahmed, Bashir, and J. Gregory Robinson. 1994. "Estimates of
Emigration of the Foreign-Born Population: 1980–1990." Technical
Working Paper No. 9. Population Division, U.S. Bureau of the
Census.

Bean, Frank D., Roland Chanove, Robert G. Cushing, Rodolfo de la
Garza, Gary Freeman, Charles W. Haynes, and David Spener. 1994.
*Illegal Mexican Migration and the United States/Mexico Border: The
Effects of Operation Hold-the-Line on El Paso/Juárez.* Report prepared
for the U.S. Commission on Immigration Reform. Austin: The
University of Texas at Austin, Population Research Center.

Bean, Frank D., Barry Edmonston, and Jeffrey S. Passel, editors. 1990.
*Undocumented Migration to the United States—IRCA and the
Experience of the 1980s.* Santa Monica, California, and Washington,
D.C.: RAND and Urban Institute.

Bean, Frank D., Thomas J. Espenshade, Michael J. White, and Robert F.
Dymowski. 1990. "Post-IRCA Changes in the Volume and

Composition of Undocumented Migration to the United States: An
Assessment Based on Apprehensions Data." In *Undocumented
Migration to the United States—IRCA and the Experience of the 1980s,*
edited by Frank D. Bean, Barry Edmonston, and Jeffrey S. Passel.
Santa Monica, California, and Washington, D.C.: RAND and Urban
Institute, pp. 111–158.

Bean, Frank D., Allan G. King, Robert D. Benford, and Laura B.
Perkinson. 1982. "Estimates of the Number of Illegal Migrants in the
State of Texas." *Texas Population Research Center Papers*, Series 4:
Paper No. 4.001.

Bean, Frank D., Allan G. King, and Jeffrey S. Passel. 1983a. "The
Number of Illegal Migrants of Mexican Origin in the United States:
Sex Ratio-Based Estimates for 1980." *Demography*, Vol. 20, pp. 99–
109.

Bean, Frank D., Allan G. King, and Jeffrey S. Passel. 1983b. "Estimates
of the Size of the Illegal Migrant Population of Mexican Origin in the
United States: An Assessment, Review, and Proposal." In *Mexican
Immigrants and Mexican Americans: An Evolving Relation*, edited by
H. Browning and R. de la Garza. Austin: CMAS Publications,
University of Texas Press, pp. 13–16.

Bean, Frank D., Georges Vernez, and Charles B. Keely. 1989. *Opening
and Closing the Doors, Evaluating Immigration Reform and Control.*
Santa Monica, California, and Washington, D.C.: RAND and Urban
Institute.

Bjerke, John A., and Karen K. Hess. 1987. "Selected Characteristics of
Illegal Aliens Apprehended by the US Border Patrol." Paper
presented at the annual meeting of the Population Association of
America, Chicago.

Borjas, George J., Richard Freeman, and Kevin Lang. 1987.
"Undocumented Mexican-Born Workers in the United States: How
Many, How Permanent?" in J. M. Abowd and R. B. Freeman, eds.,
Immigration, Trade, and the Labor Market. Chicago: University of
Chicago Press, pp. 77–100.

Boyd, Monica. 1990. "Family and Personal Networks in International
Migration: Recent Developments and New Agendas." *International
Migration Review,* Vol. 23, pp. 638–669.

Bustamante, Jorge A. 1990. "Undocumented Migration from Mexico to
the United States: Preliminary Findings of the Zapata Canyon
Project." In *Undocumented Migration to the United States—IRCA and
the Experience of the 1980s,* edited by Frank D. Bean, Barry
Edmonston, and Jeffrey S. Passel. Santa Monica, California, and
Washington, D.C.: RAND and Urban Institute, pp. 211–226.

Byerly, Edwin R. 1993. "State Population Estimates by Age and Sex:
1980 to 1992." U.S. Bureau of the Census, *Current Population
Reports,* P25-1106. U.S. Government Printing Office: Washington,
D.C.

Byerly, Edwin R., and Kevin Deardorff. 1995. "National and State
Population Estimates: 1990 to 1994." U.S. Bureau of the Census,
Current Population Reports, P25-1127, U.S. Government Printing
Office, Washington, D.C.

California Assembly Select Committee on California-Mexico Affairs.
1993. *Immigrants, Immigration, and the California Economy; A
Compendium of Materials Submitted at an Informational Hearing.*
Sacramento, California, February 25, 1993.

California Department of Finance. 1991. *Estimate of Net Foreign Migration by Category of Migrant for California Counties and the State, April 1 1980 to April 1 1990*, Report SR 91-3.

California Department of Finance. 1980–1992. *Driver License Address Change Report.* Sacramento, California.

California Department of Finance. 1992. *Notes on Driver License Address Change Report.* Sacramento, California.

California Department of Finance. 1993. *Governor's Budget 1993-1994: From Adversity to Opportunity.* Sacramento, California.

California Department of Finance. 1995. *Legal Foreign Immigration to California: Size and Characteristics of the Flow According to the INS Statistics for 1993.* Sacramento, California.

California Department of Finance. 1996. *Estimates of the Population of the State of California with Components of Change and Crude Rates, 1941–1995*, Report 95 E-7. Sacramento, California, May.

California Department of Health Services. 1993. *Vital Statistics of California, 1991.* Sacramento, California.

California Employment Development Department. 1996. *Civilian Labor Force, Employment, and Unemployment; 1980–Current (March 1994 Benchmark).* January 22.

California Senate Office of Research. 1991. *A Review of Selected Issues Relating to Undocumented Persons in San Diego.* Report Prepared for Senator William A. Craven, Chair of the Senate Special Committee on Border Issues. Sacramento, California.

California Senate Office of Research. 1993. *Californians Together: Defining the State's Role in Immigration.* Sacramento, California.

Chavez, Leo. 1988. "Settlers and Sojourners: The Case of Mexicans in the United States." *Human Organization,* Vol. 47, No. 2 (summer), pp. 95–107.

Clark, Rebecca L., and Jeffrey S. Passel. 1993. *How Much Do Immigrants Pay in Taxes? Evidence from Los Angeles County.* Washington, D.C.: The Urban Institute.

Clark, Rebecca L., Jeffrey S. Passel, Wendy N. Zimmerman, and Michael E. Fix. 1994. *Fiscal Impacts of Undocumented Aliens: Selected Estimates for Seven States.* Washington, D.C.: The Urban Institute.

Comprehensive Adult Student Assessment System. 1989. *A Survey of Newly Legalized Persons in California.* Report prepared for the California Health and Welfare Agency. San Diego, California: CASAS.

Cornelius, Wayne A. 1989. "Impacts of the 1986 U.S. Immigration Law on Emigration from Rural Mexican Sending Communities." *Population and Development Review*, Vol. 15, No. 4.

Cornelius, Wayne A. 1989–90. "Mexican Immigrants in California Today." *ISSR Working Papers in the Social Sciences* [UCLA]: Vol. 5, No. 10.

Cornelius, Wayne A. 1990. "Impacts of the 1986 U.S. Immigration Law on Emigration from Rural Mexican Sending Communities." In *Undocumented Migration to the United States—IRCA and the Experience of the 1980s*, edited by Frank D. Bean, Barry Edmonston, and Jeffrey S. Passel. Santa Monica, California, and Washington, D.C.: RAND and Urban Institute, pp. 227–250.

Cornelius, Wayne A. 1991. "Los Migrantes de la Crisis: The Changing Profile of Mexican Migration to the United States." In *Social Responses to Mexico's Economic Crisis of the 1980s*, edited by Mercedes

González de la Rocha and Agustín Escobar Latapí. San Diego, California: Center for U.S. Mexico Studies, pp. 155–193.

Crane, Keith, Beth J. Asch, Joanna Zorn Heilbrunn, and Danielle C. Cullinane. 1990. *The Effect of Employer Sanctions on the Flow of Undocumented Immigrants to the United States*. Santa Monica, California, and Washington, D.C.: RAND and Urban Institute.

Davis, Sam T. 1994. *Evaluation of Postcensal County Estimates for the 1980s*. Technical Working Paper No. 5, U.S. Bureau of the Census.

Day, Jennifer Cheeseman. 1996. "Population Projections of the United States by Age, Sex, Race, and Hispanic Origin: 1995 to 2050," U.S. Bureau of the Census, *Current Population Reports*, P25–1130, Washington, D.C.: U.S. Government Printing Office.

Donato, Katherine M. 1993. "Current Trends and Patterns of Female Migration: Evidence from Mexico." *International Migration Review*, Vol. 27, No. 4, pp. 748–771.

Donato, Katharine M., Jorge Durand, and Douglas S. Massey. 1992a. "Stemming the Tide? Assessing the Deterrent Effects of the Immigration Reform and Control Act." *Demography*, Vol. 29, pp. 139–157.

Donato, Katharine M., Jorge Durand, and Douglas S. Massey. 1992b. "Changing Conditions in the US Labor Market; Effects of the Immigration Reform and Control Act of 1986." *Population Research and Policy Review*, Vol. 11, pp. 93–115.

Donato, Katherine M., and Douglas S. Massey. 1993. "Effect of the Immigration Reform and Control Act on the Wages of Mexican Migrants." *Social Science Quarterly*, Vol. 74, pp. 523–541.

Duleep, Harriet Orcutt. 1994. "Social Security and the Emigration of Immigrants." *Social Security Bulletin*, Vol. 57, No. 1, pp. 37–52.

Edmonston, Barry, Jeffrey S. Passel, and Frank D. Bean. 1990. "Perceptions and Estimates of Undocumented Migration to the United States." In *Undocumented Migration to the United States— IRCA and the Experience of the 1980s*, edited by Frank D. Bean, Barry Edmonston, and Jeffrey S. Passel. Santa Monica, California, and Washington, D.C.: RAND and Urban Institute, pp. 11–32.

Ellis, Mark, and Richard Wright. 1996. *When Immigrants Are Not Migrants: Counting Arrivals of the Foreign Born Using the US Census.* Working Paper Series No. 2, Hanover, New Hampshire: The Nelson A. Rockefeller Center for the Social Sciences, Dartmouth College.

Espenshade, Thomas J. 1990. "Undocumented Migration to the United States: Evidence from a Repeated Trials Model." In *Undocumented Migration to the United States—IRCA and the Experience of the 1980s*, edited by Frank D. Bean, Barry Edmonston, and Jeffrey S. Passel. Santa Monica, California, and Washington, D.C.: RAND and Urban Institute, pp. 159–182.

Espenshade, Thomas J. 1992. "Policy Influences on Undocumented Migration to the United States." *Proceedings of the American Philosophical Society*, Vol. 136, No. 2.

Espenshade, Thomas J. 1994. "Does the Threat of Border Apprehension Deter Undocumented U.S. Immigration?" *Population and Development Review*, Vol. 20, pp. 871–891.

Espenshade, Thomas J. 1995. "Using INS Border Apprehension Data to Measure the Flow of Undocumented Migrants Crossing the U.S.-Mexico Frontier." *International Migration Review*, Vol. 29, No. 2.

Fawcett, James T. 1990. "Networks, Linkages, and Migration Systems." *International Migration Review*, Vol. 23, pp. 671–680.

Fay, Robert E., Jeffrey S. Passel, and J. Gregory Robinson. 1988. *The Coverage of Population in the 1980 Census.* 1980 Census of Population and Housing Evaluation and Research Reports, PHC80-E4, Washington D.C.: U.S. Department of Commerce, Bureau of the Census.

Fernandez, Edward W., and J. Gregory Robinson. 1994. "Illustrative Ranges of the Distribution of Undocumented Immigrants by State." Unpublished paper, Population Division, U.S. Bureau of the Census.

Fix, Michael, and Jeffrey S. Passel. 1994. *Immigration and Immigrants: Setting the Record Straight.* Washington D.C.: The Urban Institute.

González de la Rocha, Mercedes, and Agustín Escobar Latapí. 1990. *The Impact of IRCA on the Migration Patterns of a Community in Los Altos, Jalisco, Mexico.* Commission for the Study of International Migration and Cooperative Economic Development, Working paper No. 41.

Hanson, Gordon H., and Antonio Spilimbergo. 1996. *Illegal Immigration, Border Enforcement, and Relative Wages: Evidence from Apprehensions at the U.S.-Mexico Border.* National Bureau of Economic Research Working Paper 5592.

Heer, David M. 1990. *Undocumented Mexicans in the United States.* New York: Cambridge University Press.

Hill, Kenneth. 1985. "Illegal Aliens: An Assessment." In National Research Council, National Academy of Sciences, *Immigration Statistics: A Story of Neglect*, Report of the Panel on Immigration Statistics, Daniel B. Levine, Kenneth Hill, and Robert Warren (editors). Washington, D.C.: National Academy Press.

Hoag, Elizabeth. 1995. *New Californians: Legal Foreign Immigration to California 1992–93*. Sacramento, California: California Department of Finance.

Huddle, Donald. 1994. *The Net Costs of Immigration to California: Executive Summary*. Washington D.C.: Carrying Capacity Network.

Johnson, Hans. 1993. "Immigrants in California: Findings from the 1990 Census." California Research Bureau, Issue Summary. Sacramento: California State Library and California Department of Finance.

Johnson, Hans. 1994. "Background Report on Document Fraud Prepared for Assembly Member Grace Napolitano." Sacramento: California Research Bureau, California State Library.

Johnson, Hans, and Richard Lovelady. 1995. "Migration Between California and Other States: 1985-1994." Issue Summary CRB-IS-95-006. Sacramento: California Research Bureau and California Department of Finance.

Kossoudji, Sherrie. 1992. "Playing Cat and Mouse at the U.S.-Mexican Border." *Demography*, Vol. 29, pp. 159–180.

Kraly, Ellen Percy, and Robert Warren. 1992. "Estimates of Long-Term Immigration to the United States: Moving US Statistics toward United Nations Concepts." *Demography*, Vol. 29, No. 4, pp. 613–626.

Levine, Daniel B., Kenneth Hill, and Robert Warren, editors. 1985. *Immigration Statistics, A Story of Neglect*. Washington, D.C.: National Academy Press.

Long, John F. 1993. *Postcensal Population Estimates: States, Counties, and Places*. Population Division, U.S. Bureau of the Census, Technical Working Paper No. 3.

Los Angeles County, Internal Services Department, Urban Research Section. 1992. *Impact of Undocumented Persons and Other Immigrants on Costs, Revenues, and Services in Los Angeles County.* Report prepared for the Los Angeles County Board of Supervisors.

Lowell, B. Lindsay, and Zhongren Jing. 1994. "Unauthorized Workers and Immigration Reform: What Can We Ascertain from Employers?" *International Migration Review*, Vol. 28, No. 3, pp. 427–429.

Martin, John L. 1995. *How Many Illegal Immigrants?* Center for Immigration Studies Backgrounder, No. 4-95, September.

Martin, Philip. 1990a. "The Mexican Crisis and Mexico-US Migration." Unpublished paper.

Martin, Philip L. 1990b. "Harvest of Confusion: Immigration Reform and California Agriculture." *International Migration Review*, Vol. 24, No. 1, pp. 69–95.

Martin, Philip L. 1993. *Trade and Migration: NAFTA and Agriculture.* Washington, D.C.: Institute for International Economics.

Martin, Philip L. 1994. "Good Intentions Gone Awry: IRCA and U.S. Agriculture." *ANNALS, AAPSS*, Vol. 534, pp. 44–57.

Massey, Douglas S., Joaquin Arango, Graeme Hugo, Ali Kouaoci, Adela Pellegrino, and J. Edward Taylor. 1994. "An Evaluation of International Migration Theory: The North American Case." *Population and Development Review*, Vol. 20, No. 4, pp. 699–751.

Massey, Douglas S., Katherine M. Donato, and Zai Liang. 1990. "Effects of the Immigration Reform and Control Act of 1986: Preliminary Data from Mexico." In *Undocumented Migration to the United States—IRCA and the Experience of the 1980s*, edited by Frank D. Bean, Barry Edmonston, and Jeffrey S. Passel. Santa Monica,

California, and Washington, D.C.: RAND and Urban Institute, pp. 183–210.

Massey, Douglas S., and Felipe Garcia Espaqa. 1987. "The Social Process of International Migration." *Science*, Vol. 237, pp. 733–738.

Massey, Douglas S., Luin Goldring, and Jorge Durand. 1994. "Continuities in Transnational Migration: An Analysis of Nineteen Mexican Communities." *American Journal of Sociology*, Vol. 99, No. 6, pp. 1492–1533.

Massey, Douglas S., and Audrey Singer. 1995. "New Estimates of Undocumented Mexican Migration and the Probability of Apprehension." *Demography*, Vol. 32, No. 2, pp. 203–213.

Migration News, Vol. 3, No. 6, June 1996.

Mincer, Jacob. 1978. "Family Migration Decisions." *Journal of Political Economy*, Vol. 86, pp. 749–773.

Muller, T., and T. J. Espenshade. 1985. *The Fourth Wave: California's Newest Immigrants.* Washington, D.C.: Urban Institute Press.

Parker, Richard A., and Louis M. Rea. 1993. "Illegal Immigration in San Diego County: An Analysis of Costs and Revenues." Report to the California State Senate Special Committee on Border Issues. Sacramento: California Legislature.

Parker, Theresa A. 1994. "The California Story: Immigrants Come to California as a Result of Federal—not State—Policies." *Public Welfare*, Vol. 52, pp. 16–20.

Passel, Jeffrey S. 1985. "Undocumented Immigrants: How Many?" *Proceedings of the Social Statistics Section*, American Statistical Association, Washington, D.C., pp. 65–72.

Passel, Jeffrey S., Frank D. Bean, and Barry Edmonston. 1990. "Undocumented Migration Since IRCA: An Overall Assessment." In

Undocumented Migration to the United States—IRCA and the Experience of the 1980s, edited by Frank D. Bean, Barry Edmonston, and Jeffrey S. Passel. Santa Monica, California, and Washington, D.C.: RAND and Urban Institute, pp. 251–266.

Passel, Jeffrey S., and Karen A. Woodrow. 1984. "Geographic Distribution of Undocumented Aliens Counted in the 1980 Census by States," *International Migration Review*, Vol. 18 (Fall), No. 3, pp. 642–671.

Passel, Jeffrey S., and Karen A. Woodrow. 1985. "Change in the Undocumented Alien Population in the United States, 1979-1983." Revised version of a paper presented at the annual meeting of the Population Association of America, Boston.

Rasmussen, Nelson. 1974. "The Use of Driver License Address Change Records for Estimating Interstate and Intercounty Migration." Paper presented at the Small Area Statistics Conference, St. Louis, Missouri.

Rea, Louis M., and Richard A. Parker. 1992. *A Fiscal Impact Analysis of Undocumented Immigrants Residing in San Diego County.* Sacramento: Office of the Auditor General of California.

Robinson, J. Gregory, and Bashir Ahmed. 1992. "Utility of Synthetic Estimates of Census Coverage for States Based on National Demographic Analysis Estimates." Paper presented at the annual meeting of the Population Association of America, Denver, 1992.

Robinson, J. Gregory, Bashir Ahmed, Pritwis Das Gupta, Karen A. Woodrow. 1991. "Estimating Coverage of the 1990 United States Census: Demographic Analysis." *Proceedings of the Social Statistics Section*, American Statistical Association.

Romero, Phillip J., and Andrew J. Chang. 1994. *Shifting the Costs of a Failed Federal Policy: The Net Fiscal Impact of Illegal Immigrants in*

California. Sacramento, California: Governor's Office of Planning and Research and California Department of Finance.

Rothman, Eric S., and Thomas J. Espenshade. 1992. "Fiscal Impacts of Immigration to the United States." *Population Index,* Vol. 58, pp. 381-415.

Taylor, J. Edward. 1993. "Worker Turnover, Farm Labor Contractors, and IRCA's Impact on the California Farm Labor Market." *American Journal of Agricultural Economics,* Vol. 75, pp. 350–360.

U.S. Bureau of the Census. 1994. *Statistical Abstract of the United States: 1994 (114th edition.).* Washington, D.C.

U.S. Bureau of the Census. 1995. "The Foreign-Born Population: 1994." *Current Population Reports,* P20-486, August.

U.S. Bureau of the Census. 1996. "Methodology for Estimates of State and County Total Population (used for 1990 to 1994 estimates)." Extracted from Report P25-1127. Downloaded from World Wide Web site: http://www.census.gov/ftp/pub/population/methods/stco.txt.

U.S. Commission on Agricultural Workers. 1992. *Report of the Commission on Agricultural Workers.* Washington, D.C.: Government Printing Office.

U.S. Commission on Immigration Reform. 1994. *Prepared Statement of Barbara Jordan, Chair, U.S. Commission on Immigration Reform before the Subcommittee on Immigration and Refugee Affairs Committee on the Judiciary, U.S. Senate,* Washington D.C., August 3.

U.S. Commission on Immigration Reform. 1995. *Statement of Barbara Jordan, Chair, U.S. Commission on Immigration Reform before the Subcommittee on Immigration and Refugee Affairs Committee on the Judiciary, U.S. Senate,* Washington D.C., June.

U.S. Congress, House of Representatives Committee on the Judiciary. 1986. *Immigration Reform and Control Act of 1986.* Conference Report, 99th Congress, 2nd Session, Report 99-1000, October 14.

U.S. Department of Justice, Immigration and Naturalization Service. 1990. *1989 Statistical Yearbook of the Immigration and Naturalization Service,* September.

U.S. Department of Justice, Immigration and Naturalization Service. 1992. *Immigration Reform and Control Act: Report on the Legalized Alien Population.*

U.S. Department of Labor. 1993. *U.S. Farmworkers in the Post-IRCA Period.* U.S. Department of Labor Research Report No. 4, March.

U.S. General Accounting Office. 1993. *Illegal Aliens: Despite Data Limitations, Current Methods Provide Better Population Estimates.* Report to the Chairman, Information, Justice, Transportation and Agriculture Subcommittee, Committee on Government Operations, House of Representatives, GAO/PEMD-93-25, August.

U.S. General Accounting Office. 1994. *Illegal Aliens: Assessing Estimates of Financial Burden on California.* Report to the Honorable Barbara Boxer, U.S. Senate, GAO/HEHS-95-22, November.

U.S. General Accounting Office. 1995a. *Illegal Immigration: INS Overstay Methods Need Improvement.* GAO/PEMD-95-20, September.

U.S. General Accounting Office. 1995b. *Illegal Aliens: National Net Cost Estimates Vary Widely.* Letter Report, GAO/HEHS-95-133.

U.S. Immigration and Naturalization Service. 1989. *International Migration to the United States.* The President's Comprehensive Triennial Report on Immigration, 1989, 1-31. Washington, D.C.: U.S. Government Printing Office.

U.S. Internal Revenue Service. 1995. *IRS Area to Area Migration and County Income Data.* Statistics of Income Division, April.

Warren, Robert. 1990. "Annual Estimates of Nonimmigrant Overstays in the United States: 1985 to 1988." In *Undocumented Migration to the United States—IRCA and the Experience of the 1980s*, edited by Frank D. Bean, Barry Edmonston, and Jeffrey S. Passel. Santa Monica, California, and Washington, D.C.: RAND and Urban Institute, pp. 77–110.

Warren, Robert. 1994. "Estimates of the Unauthorized Immigrant Population Residing in the United States, by Country of Origin and State of Residence: October 1992." Unpublished report, U.S. Immigration and Naturalization Service.

Warren, Robert, and Ellen Percy Kraly. 1985. *The Elusive Exodus: Emigration from the United States.* Population Trends and Public Policy Occasional Paper No. 8. Washington, D.C.: Population Reference Bureau.

Warren, Robert, and Jeffrey S. Passel. 1987. "A Count of the Uncountable: Estimates of Undocumented Aliens Counted in the 1980 United States Census." *Demography*, Vol. 24, No. 3, pp. 375–393.

Woodrow, Karen A. 1990. "Undocumented Immigrants Living in the United States." Paper presented at the annual meetings of the American Statistical Association, Anaheim, California.

Woodrow, Karen A. 1992. "A Consideration of the Effect of Immigration Reform on the Number of Undocumented Residents in the United States." *Population Research and Policy Review*, Vol. 11, pp. 117–144.

Woodrow, Karen A., and Jeffrey S. Passel. 1989. *Estimates of Emigration Based on Sample Survey Data from Resident Relatives.* Report prepared for the Office of Information and Regulatory Affairs, Office of Management and Budget. Washington, D.C.: U.S. Bureau of the Census, April.

Woodrow, Karen A., and Jeffrey S. Passel. 1990. "Post-IRCA Undocumented Immigration to the United States: An Assessment Based on the June 1988 CPS." In *Undocumented Migration to the United States—IRCA and the Experience of the 1980s,* edited by Frank D. Bean, Barry Edmonston, and Jeffrey S. Passel. Santa Monica, California, and Washington, D.C.: RAND and Urban Institute, pp. 33–76.

Woodrow, Karen A., Jeffrey S. Passel, and Robert Warren. 1987. "Preliminary Estimates of Undocumented Immigration to the United States, 1980-1986: Analysis of the June 1986 Current Population Survey." *Proceedings of the Social Statistics Section of the American Statistical Association Meeting,* San Francisco.

Woodrow-Lafield, Karen A. 1994. "Potential Sponsorship by IRCA-Legalized Immigrants." U.S. Commission on Immigration Reform, Research Paper.

Woodrow-Lafield, Karen A. 1995. "An Analysis of Net Immigration in Census Coverage Evaluation." *Population Research and Policy Review,* Vol. 14, pp. 173–204.

Woodrow-Lafield, Karen A. 1996a. "Emigration from the USA: Multiplicity Survey Evidence." *Population Research and Policy Review,* Vol. 15, pp. 171–199.

Woodrow-Lafield, Karen A. 1996b. "In Search of a Method: Judgment and the Problem of Estimating Unknown Migration." Unpublished paper.

Word, David L. 1992. *The Census Bureau Approach for Allocating Internal Migration to States, Counties and Places: 1981–1991.* Population Estimates and Projections Technical Working Paper Series, Report Number 1, U.S. Bureau of the Census.

About the Author

HANS P. JOHNSON

Hans P. Johnson is a research fellow at the Public Policy Institute of California. His research interests include international and domestic migration, population estimates and projections, and state and local demography. He was previously the senior demographer at the California Research Bureau, where he conducted research for the State Legislature and Governor's Office on population issues, authoring several publications on migration. He has also worked as a demographer at the California Department of Finance, specializing in population projections.

Johnson received his B.S. in business administration and M.A. in biostatistics from the University of California, Berkeley. He is currently working on his dissertation in demography at the University of California, Berkeley.